Environment at a Glance 2020

OECD

BETTER POLICIES FOR BETTER LIVES

This work is published under the responsibility of the Secretary-General of the OECD. The opinions expressed and arguments employed herein do not necessarily reflect the official views of OECD member countries.

This document, as well as any data and map included herein, are without prejudice to the status of or sovereignty over any territory, to the delimitation of international frontiers and boundaries and to the name of any territory, city or area.

The statistical data for Israel are supplied by and under the responsibility of the relevant Israeli authorities. The use of such data by the OECD is without prejudice to the status of the Golan Heights, East Jerusalem and Israeli settlements in the West Bank under the terms of international law.

Note by Turkey
The information in this document with reference to "Cyprus" relates to the southern part of the Island. There is no single authority representing both Turkish and Greek Cypriot people on the Island. Turkey recognises the Turkish Republic of Northern Cyprus (TRNC). Until a lasting and equitable solution is found within the context of the United Nations, Turkey shall preserve its position concerning the "Cyprus issue".

Note by all the European Union Member States of the OECD and the European Union
The Republic of Cyprus is recognised by all members of the United Nations with the exception of Turkey. The information in this document relates to the area under the effective control of the Government of the Republic of Cyprus.

Please cite this publication as:
OECD (2020), *Environment at a Glance 2020*, OECD Publishing, Paris, https://doi.org/10.1787/4ea7d35f-en.

ISBN 978-92-64-49855-6 (print)
ISBN 978-92-64-91625-8 (pdf)

Environment at a Glance
ISSN 1995-414X (print)
ISSN 1996-4064 (online)

Photo credits:
Cover © Mike Pellinni/Shutterstock.com.

Corrigenda to publications may be found on line at:
www.oecd.org/about/publishing/corrigenda.htm.

Tuscany landscape in early morning mist
Photo © Martin Mecnarowski/Shutterstock.com

ENVIRONMENT AT A GLANCE 2020

Sea level continues to rise at a rate of about
3.2 millimetres per year
Photo © Sascha Christian/Shutterstock.com

Preface

Environment at a Glance 2020 presents the progress made by OECD countries in reducing greenhouse gas emissions, improving air quality, protecting natural habitats, and improving the management of waste and freshwater resources. It reveals where progress has slowed or is still insufficient. Climate change is occurring faster than expected and biodiversity loss is occurring at an alarming rate in several countries. Air pollution continues to affect human health. Short-lived climate pollutants, pharmaceuticals in freshwater and plastics in the environment raise new and growing concerns. Public pressure for action on climate change and other environmental issues is mounting. Policies still lack coherence, undermining efforts to reduce negative environmental impacts in the long run.

I see substantial scope for strengthening air and climate policies, changing patterns of energy consumption, preserving biodiversity and natural resources, applying an integrated life-cycle approach to materials management, better aligning policies, and reinforcing institutions and multilateral cooperation – all critical components of sustainable development. At a time when many countries have to cope with economic challenges and painful trade-offs, this tests governments and businesses alike.

To be effective, policies need to be based on sound and reliable information. Governments, decision makers and civil society need to know how their country is performing, over time and compared to other countries. The OECD works closely with countries and international partners to improve the quality of information on the environment and sustainable development. We support countries in monitoring their progress, improving their environmental information systems, and producing reliable and coherent indicators.

It is also the OECD's task to provide governments and the public at large with internationally harmonised data and indicators on the environment. I am proud of our new interactive online platform where users can find the indicators used in this report, updated in real-time from the OECD's databases, and tailor them to their own needs. It is our plan to progressively expand this "Environment at a Glance" platform to other topics and indicators, and to make it a user-friendly gateway to all OECD environmental and green growth indicators. I very much hope you will find it helpful and I look forward to seeing your feedback.

Rodolfo Lacy
Director, OECD Environment Directorate

Foreword

This report is part of the OECD Programme on Environmental Information and Indicators steered by the Working Party on Environmental Information (WPEI) of the OECD Environment Policy Committee.

The aim of this programme is to develop objective, reliable and comparable information on the environment and sustainable development for use in international work, and to support countries in their efforts to improve environmental information systems and establish effective mechanisms to inform the public and decision makers. The OECD has long advocated better environmental information, including appropriate and free access to it. Its work has been instrumental in the use of coherent frameworks for environmental data and reporting, environmental indicators, and more recently green growth indicators. The OECD is part of global efforts to implement and further develop the System of Environmental and Economic Accounts and monitors well-being and inclusive growth.

The data and indicators used in this report are regularly updated and available on the new interactive Environment at a Glance web-platform. They have been compiled through a cooperative process involving country representatives in the WPEI and other international sources. This has ensured that the indicators have wide ownership in capitals and also contribute to monitoring progress towards the associated Sustainable Development Goals. Ministries and statistical offices in countries provided invaluable support for the preparation of the interactive platform.

This report was prepared by Myriam Linster and Sarah Miet of the Environment Directorate, with contributions from Carla Bertuzzi, Miguel Cárdenas Rodríguez, Assia Elgouacem, Tess Glinert, Ivan Haščič, Alexander Mackie, Mark Mateo and Mauro Migotto. Nathalie Girouard, Head of the OECD Environmental Performance and Information Division, provided oversight and guidance. Natasha Cline-Thomas, Beth Del Bourgo and Stephanie Simonin-Edwards provided editorial and communications support. Andrew Esson from Baseline Arts Ltd. designed the report. Thibaut Dufour and the team at Check-in Films produced the thematic videos. The report, the associated web-books and the web-platform benefitted from comments from colleagues in the Environment Directorate, including Ruben Bibas, Peter Börkey, Nils Axel Braathen, Adrienne Cuffley, Kathleen Dominique, Jane Ellis, Katia Karousakis, Elisa Lanzi, Frithjof Laubinger, Hannah Leckie, Xavier Leflaive, and Mikaela Rambali.

The authors are grateful to colleagues from the Public Affairs and Communications Directorate who provided technical and editorial support for the establishment of the interactive Environment at a Glance web-platform and its thematic web-books including Pascale Cissokho Mutter, who led the project, Eileen Capponi, Jonathan Dayot, Frédérique Lamoitte, Vincent Finat-Duclos, Vincent Gallart, Audrey Garrigoux, Matthias Rumpf, Janine Treves, Claudia Tromboni, and Catherine Bremer (media relations). The authors wish to acknowledge the valuable support of Anthony Cox, Environment Deputy Director and Amy Plantin, Executive Secretary of EPOC who ensured that the project received the resources needed for its successful delivery.

Lastly, special thanks are extended to Rodolfo Lacy, OECD Environment Director, for spearheading the transformation of *Environment at a Glance* from a publication into an open access digital platform. His vision and support were indispensable for the completion of the project.

Climate scientists gather data on the melting Antarctic ice cap
Photo © Stu Shaw/Shutterstock.com

CONTENTS

Wind turbines in Oresund, Denmark
Photo © Eugene Suslo/Shutterstock.com

FIGURES

BOXES

EXECUTIVE SUMMARY

Our way of life and its production and consumption patterns, put the environment, its natural resources and ecosystems under high pressure. How does this pressure evolve over time? How successful are we in breaking the link between economic growth and environmental degradation? The picture that emerges from OECD environmental indicators is mixed at best.

While countries progressed in several areas, environmental pressures remain high and much remains to be done

Some progress has been made in reducing emissions of greenhouse gases and traditional air pollutants, energy intensity, water use, municipal waste management and in improving sewage treatment and the protection of natural habitats. This can partly be attributed to structural changes in the economy and the displacement of resource- and pollution-intensive production abroad, and partly to technological progress and policy action. The slowdown in economic activity following the 2008 economic crisis also played a role.

Carbon emissions remain generally tied to economic activity and energy use; fossil fuels dominate the energy mix and countries continue to support their production and consumption, at a cost of more than USD 80 billion per year in the OECD area alone. The use of material resources to support economic growth remains high; and many valuable materials continue to be disposed of as waste. This suggests important opportunities for aligning policies and achieving environmental goals more cost-effectively.

Stronger policies are needed to improve environmental performance and establish circular and resource-efficient economies

OECD countries use a mix of instruments to address environmental pressures, including taxation to influence consumer behaviour and internalise environmental costs. But too often policies lack coherence, undermining efforts to reduce negative environmental impacts and impeding the transition to a low-carbon and resource-efficient economy.

Stronger and predictable policies are needed to effectively decouple environmental pressures from economic growth, protect and restore ecosystems, manage natural assets in a sustainable manner, prevent waste from being generated, and address new concerns, such as pharmaceutical residues in freshwater, black carbon and plastic waste. This involves proper price signals and the elimination of environmentally harmful financial support, and a long-term vision to sustain economic development and well-being.

Stronger efforts are needed to improve information to assess countries' environmental performance and track progress towards

Sustainable green buildings in Milan
Photo © Federico Rostagno/ Shutterstock.com

environment-related Sustainable Development Goals. In many areas, data are weak or missing; the absence of reliable time series makes it difficult to monitor policy outcomes, and insufficient data harmonisation across countries hampers the exchange of lessons from policy implementation.

Efforts to mitigate carbon emissions are insufficient to limit long-term increases in global temperatures

Global emissions of GHG continue to grow, mainly driven by fossil energy use. Energy-related CO_2 emissions in the OECD area have risen again in 2018, after several years of rather stable and even declining trends. OECD countries emit more CO_2 per inhabitant than other countries in the world, and their carbon footprint is generally higher than domestic emissions.

Improvements in air quality are modest

Emissions of major air pollutants have been decreasing for the OECD as a whole, and have been decoupled from economic growth in almost all countries. Emissions of sulphur oxides (SOx) and nitrogen oxides (NO_x) decreased on average by -51% and -32% respectively since 2000. In most countries for which data are available, emissions of fine particulates (PM2.5) have been decreasing thanks to optimised combustion processes, reduced use of coal, and lower emissions from transport and agriculture. Human exposure to PM2.5 has consequently decreased as did the associated welfare costs. In two out of three member countries, inhabitants are however still exposed to levels above the WHO guideline value.

Many countries face seasonal or local water stress

Globally, pressures on freshwater resources continue to mount, and competition for access to water is increasing. In most OECD countries, however, freshwater abstractions from renewable resources have decoupled from economic and population growth, and the average level of water stress has diminished since 2000 thanks to more efficient use, better pricing policies and greater exploitation of alternative water sources. Results however vary within and among countries. Very few countries experience medium-to-high water stress, but most face seasonal or local water quantity problems. A more thorough analysis is difficult; the information available remains insufficient.

Ensuring adequate sewage treatment in small or isolated settlements is still a challenge

Sewage treatment infrastructure and the provision of wastewater treatment services have improved in the OECD area since 2000. In more than one third of the countries over 80% of the inhabitants are connected to a sewage treatment plant with at least secondary treatment. Challenges remain as regards the upgrading of existing sewage networks and treatment infrastructure, servicing small and isolated settlements with adequate treatment, and ensuring proper control of small independent treatment facilities.

Material consumption remains high and the material footprint is growing

Global demand for raw materials has been rising over the past decades driven by industrialisation and infrastructure development in emerging economies, continued high levels of material consumption in high-income countries and a growing world population. The amount of materials extracted globally doubled between 1980 and 2010, and is projected to double again by 2060. OECD countries are moving towards a higher material productivity and a lower material consumption per capita. But consumption levels remain high compared to other world regions, and progress is more modest when considering the material footprint.

Many valuable materials continue to be disposed of as waste

The amounts of materials ending up as waste continue to grow in most OECD countries;. Developments are slightly more positive for municipal waste whose growth rate slowed down in the 2000s. A person living in the OECD area generates on average 520 kg of municipal waste per year; this is 30 kg less than in 2000, but still 20 kg more than in 1990. More and more waste is fed back into the economy through recycling, but landfilling remains the major disposal method in many OECD countries and many materials get recycled into low value products.

Threats to biodiversity from land use change and infrastructure development are increasing

Protected areas are expanding in all OECD countries; they cover on average 16% of land and 25% of marine areas (compared to respectively 11% and 5% in 2000). At the same time, threats to biodiversity, particularly from land use change and infrastructure development, are increasing. Land covered by buildings has increased by 15% in the OECD area since 2000; it represents about 290 km^2 per inhabitant, 3 times the world average. The highest built-up rate is found in OECD Europe. Many forests are threatened by degradation, fragmentation and conversion to other land types. Many animal and plant species in OECD countries are endangered, particularly in countries that are densely populated. Amphibians and freshwater fish are on average most threatened, but specialist birds have declined by nearly 30% in 40 years. A third of global marine fish stocks are overexploited.

Reader's guide

This report presents a digest of major environmental trends in OECD countries in areas such as climate change, air quality, biodiversity, water resources and circular economy. The analysis and key messages are based on indicators from the OECD Core Set of Environmental Indicators – a tool to monitor environmental progress and performance and to track the course towards sustainable development. It builds on the interactive Environment at a Glance web-based platform launched on 18 November 2019.

The "Environment at a Glance" interactive online platform: a gateway to OECD indicators

The Environment at a Glance platform provides an interactive access to OECD environmental indicators and to the latest data on the environment received from OECD members and compiled from international sources. It highlights major environmental trends in areas such as climate change, biodiversity, water resources, air quality, circular economy and ocean (forthcoming). Users can access the indicators updated in real-time from OECD databases, play with the data and graphics, and consult and download thematic web-books. The topics covered and the indicators provided will be progressively expanded so as to provide a user-friendly gateway to OECD indicators on the environment, green growth and sustainable development: **http://www.oecd.org/environment/ environment-at-a-glance/.**

Comparability and interpretation

The indicators used in this report are of varying relevance for different countries. Care should be taken when interpreting the indicators and when making international comparisons:

- National averages can mask significant variations within countries.

- Definitions and measurement methods vary among countries, hence inter-country comparisons may not compare the same things.

- There is a level of uncertainty associated with the data sources and measurement methods on which the indicators rely. Differences between two countries' indicators are thus not always statistically significant; and when countries are clustered around a relatively narrow range of outcomes, it may be misleading to establish an order of ranking.

- No single approach has been used for normalising the indicators; different denominators are used in parallel to balance the message conveyed. Many indicators are expressed on a per capita and per unit of GDP basis. The population estimates used include persons who are resident in a country for one year or more, regardless of their citizenship. The GDP figures used are expressed in USD and in 2010 prices and purchasing power parities (PPPs).

Definitions and metadata can be found in the web-books available at http://www.oecd.org/environment/ environment-at-a-glance/.

Cut-off date

The indicators build on the latest comparable data received from OECD members using an OECD questionnaire, and on data available from other OECD and international sources up to September 2019. Some indicators were updated on the basis of international information available in October 2019 and on the basis of comments from national delegates to the OECD Working Party on Environmental Information received by mid-October 2019.

Aggregates and abbreviations

COUNTRY AGGREGATES

OECD America   Includes the following OECD members: Canada, Chile*, Mexico and the United States.

OECD Europe   Includes all European OECD members, i.e. Austria, Belgium, the Czech Republic, Denmark, Estonia,* Finland, France, Germany, Greece, Hungary, Iceland, Ireland, Italy, Latvia,* Lithuania,* Luxembourg, the Netherlands, Norway, Poland, Portugal, the Slovak Republic, Slovenia,* Spain, Sweden, Switzerland, Turkey and the United Kingdom.

OECD Asia-Oceania   This zone includes the following member countries of the OECD: Australia, Israel*, Japan, Korea and New Zealand

OECD   This zone includes all member countries of the OECD, i.e. countries of OECD America plus countries of OECD Asia-Oceania and countries of OECD Europe.

* Chile has been a member of the OECD since 7 May 2010, Slovenia since 21 July 2010, Estonia since 9 December 2010, Israel since 7 September 2010, Latvia since 1 July 2016 and Lithuania since 5 July 2018.

Country aggregates may include Secretariat estimates.

ABBREVIATIONS

CFCs	Chlorofluorocarbons	PM10	Small particulate matter, smaller than 10 microns in diameter
CH_4	Methane		
CO_2	Carbon dioxide	PPP	Purchasing power parities
DMC	Domestic material consumption	SCBD	Secretariat of the Convention on Biological Diversity
EEA	European Environment Agency		
EEZ	Exclusive economic zone	SF_6	Sulphur hexafluoride
EU	European Union	SO_x	Sulphur oxides
FAO	Food and Agriculture Organization of the United Nations	SO_2	Sulphur dioxide
		TPES	Total primary energy supply µg microgram
G20	Group of Twenty (19 countries and the EU)	UNEP	UN Environment Programme
GDP	Gross domestic product	UNESCO	United Nations Educational, Scientific and Cultural Organization
GHG	Greenhouse gas		
HFCs	Hydrofluorocarbons	UNFCCC	UN Framework Convention on Climate Change
IEA	International Energy Agency	UNSD	United Nations Statistics Division
IUCN	International Union for Conservation of Nature	USD	US dollar
m^3	Cubic meter	WHO	World Health Organization
NO_x	Nitrogen oxides	WMO	World Meteorological Organization
NO_2	Nitrogen dioxide	WWAP	World Water Assessment Programme
N_2O	Nitrous oxide		
PFC	Perfluorocarbons		
PM	Particulate matter		
PM2.5	Fine particulate matter, smaller than 2.5 microns in diameter		

1 CLIMATE CHANGE

Emissions of greenhouse gases from human activities disturb the radiative energy balance of the earth-atmosphere system, leading to temperature changes and other disruptions of the earth's climate. Climate change affects ecosystems, water resources, food production, human settlements and the frequency and scale of extreme weather events with significant consequences for human well-being and economic output.

Progress is measured through indicators on greenhouse gas and carbon emissions, developments in energy supply and energy intensity, the share of renewable energy sources in the supply mix, and fossil fuel subsidies.

Climate change affects ecosystems
Photo © Sepp photography/Shutterstock.com

THE ISSUE

Emissions of greenhouse gases (GHGs) from human activities disturb the radiative energy balance of the earth-atmosphere system. They exacerbate the natural greenhouse effect, leading to temperature changes and other disruptions of the earth's climate. Most emissions stem from energy use in transport, industry and by households. Agriculture, forestry and land use changes also play a role by altering carbon sinks. Carbon dioxide (CO_2) from the combustion of fossil fuels and deforestation is a major contributor to greenhouse gases and a key factor in countries' ability to mitigate climate change. National emissions are also affected by changes in global demand and supply patterns with increasing trade flows and the displacement of carbon-intensive production abroad. Reductions in domestic emissions can thus be partially or wholly offset elsewhere in the world.

Climate change is of global concern for its effects on green growth and sustainable development. It threatens ecosystems and biodiversity, affects water resources, human settlements and changes the frequency and scale of extreme weather events, with consequences for food production, economic output and human well-being.

POLICY CHALLENGES

The main challenges are to mitigate GHG emissions and stabilise GHG concentrations in the atmosphere at a level that would limit dangerous interference with the climate system, and to adapt to and manage risks from climate change.

This implies implementing national and international low-carbon strategies and further decoupling GHG emissions from economic growth. It also implies increasing the share of renewable energy sources in the supply mix, and improving energy intensity by adopting energy-efficient production processes and increasing the energy efficiency

CO$_2$ from the combustion of fossil fuels and deforestation is a major contributor to greenhouse gases and a key factor in countries' ability to mitigate climate change.

of consumer goods and services. With the increasing interdependence of global value chains, domestic mitigation efforts must be placed in a global context and build on a good understanding of carbon flows associated with international trade and final domestic demand.

Ensuring a proper mix of market-based instruments, for example by promoting carbon pricing, environmentally-related taxation and removing government subsidies and other support for fossil fuels, and providing access to climate finance play an important role in this transition. Governments must also align policies across a diverse range of non-climate areas including transport, housing, construction, spatial planning, agriculture and development cooperation. And they must consider synergies between emission reduction, adaptation strategies and broader well-being objectives, such as reduced air pollution and improved health. The impact of climate policies on issues such as the affordability of energy and jobs also needs to be taken into account to counter economic and social inequalities within and between countries.

MEASURING PERFORMANCE AND PROGRESS

Environmental performance can be evaluated against domestic objectives and international goals and commitments.

Tackling climate change is part of the 2030 Agenda for Sustainable Development (New York, September 2015) under Goal 13 *"Take urgent action to combat climate change and its impacts"*. Targets supporting climate action are included under Goal 12 *"Ensure sustainable consumption and production patterns"*, Goal 9 *"Build resilient infrastructure, promote inclusive and sustainable industrialization and foster innovation"*, and Goal 7 *"Ensure access to affordable, reliable, sustainable and modern energy for all"*.

The main international agreement is the United Nations Framework Convention on Climate Change (1992) which is the basis of:

- The Kyoto Protocol (1997) that set internationally binding and differentiated emission reduction targets for six GHGs for 2008-12. It has been ratified by 177 parties, including all but two OECD countries, and has been in force since 2005. 37 industrialised countries and the European Union committed to reduce GHG emissions by an average of 5% below 1990 levels. The "Doha Amendment to the Kyoto Protocol" (2012), includes new commitments for the period 2013-20 and a revised list of GHGs. Parties committed to reduce GHG emissions by an average of at least 18% below 1990 levels over 2013-20. The amendment is not yet in force.

- The Paris Agreement (2015) that strengthens the global response to climate change. The objective is to keep the average global temperature rise this century well below 2 degrees Celsius and as close as possible to 1.5 degrees Celsius above pre-industrial levels. Parties have expressed their commitments to 2025 or 2030 through nationally determined contributions (NDCs), including a regular report on their emissions and implementation efforts.

This is supported by the commitment in 2009 of the Leaders of the Group of Twenty (G20) economies to "phase out and rationalize over the medium term inefficient fossil fuel subsidies while providing targeted support for the poorest". To follow up on this commitment, members of the G20 have since engaged in a voluntary process of periodically reporting on their fossil-fuel subsidies.

MAIN TRENDS AND RECENT DEVELOPMENTS

GHG emissions are growing worldwide, but have stabilised in the OECD area

GHG emissions continue to grow in many countries and worldwide. Historically, OECD countries emitted the bulk of global CO_2 and other GHGs. But since 1990, emissions

---

┌─ **KEY MESSAGES ON CLIMATE CHANGE** ─────────

- Global emissions of greenhouse gases (GHG) continue to grow. They have increased by 50% since 1990, and by 35% since 2000, driven by economic growth and fossil energy use. In the OECD area however, the growth rate of GHG emissions has been slowing down since 2007 and emissions even decreased, partly due to the economic slowdown following the 2008 financial crisis, but also to strengthened climate policies.

- Today, OECD countries emit about 35% of global CO_2 emissions from energy use, compared to more than 50% in 1990 and to 47% in 2005. A more nuanced picture emerges when considering emissions along global value chains. The carbon footprint of OECD countries that accounts for all carbon emitted anywhere in the world to satisfy domestic final demand is about 18% higher than domestic emissions.

- Overall progress is insufficient. Climate change is occurring faster than expected and GHG emissions in OECD countries could rise again due to an increase in energy-related CO_2 emissions in 2018.

- Important drivers behind these trends are economic growth and fossil energy use. Energy intensity decreased for OECD countries overall, but results to date are insufficient to effectively reduce GHG emissions from energy use. Renewables play a small, though growing, role in energy mixes. OECD countries continue to rely on fossil fuels for about 80% of their energy supply, and many governments continue to support fossil fuel production and use financially, in particular oil and gas. In 2017, OECD countries provided around USD 80 billion of such support. This is 26% less than the highest amount in 2013. But progress in recent years has been slowing.

───

in OECD countries have grown at a slower pace than emissions in other world regions, reducing the OECD's share in global emissions. The share of other world regions has been growing in particular since the early 2000s pushed by economic growth and increasing use of fossil energy in developing countries. CO_2 from the combustion of fossil fuels and biomass and industrial processes determines the overall trend; it represents more than 70% of global GHG emissions; together with CH_4 and N_2O, it reaches 98% (IEA, 2019).

At global level

- GHG emissions have grown by 50% since 1990, and 35% since 2000.

- CO_2 emissions from energy use have grown by 60% since 1990, and 41% since 2000. After three years of stability they rose again in 2017, reaching a record high of 32 billion tonnes.

In OECD countries

- GHG emissions have grown by 4% since 1990, and have fallen by 6% since 2000.

- CO_2 emissions from energy use have grown by 5% since 1990, and have fallen by 8% since 2000.

Today, OECD countries emit about 35% of global CO_2 emissions from energy use, compared to more than 50% in 1990 and 47% in 2005.

OECD countries however still emit far more CO_2 per inhabitant than most other world regions, i.e. an average of 9 tonnes of CO_2 per capita, compared to 4 tonnes in the rest of the world. Average per capita amounts have hardly changed since 1990.

GHG emissions of OECD countries peaked in 2007 and have fallen by 9% since then. This reflects strengthened climate policies, changing patterns of energy consumption and gains in energy efficiency. It also reflects a slowdown in economic activity following the 2008 economic crisis. Emission intensities both per unit of GDP and per capita have been decreasing since 2000 in almost all OECD countries, revealing a decoupling from economic growth. Most OECD countries met their emission reduction commitments for 2008-12 under the Kyoto Protocol and are on track to meet their 2020 target.

Figure 1. Carbon emissions have grown at a slower pace in OECD countries than globally

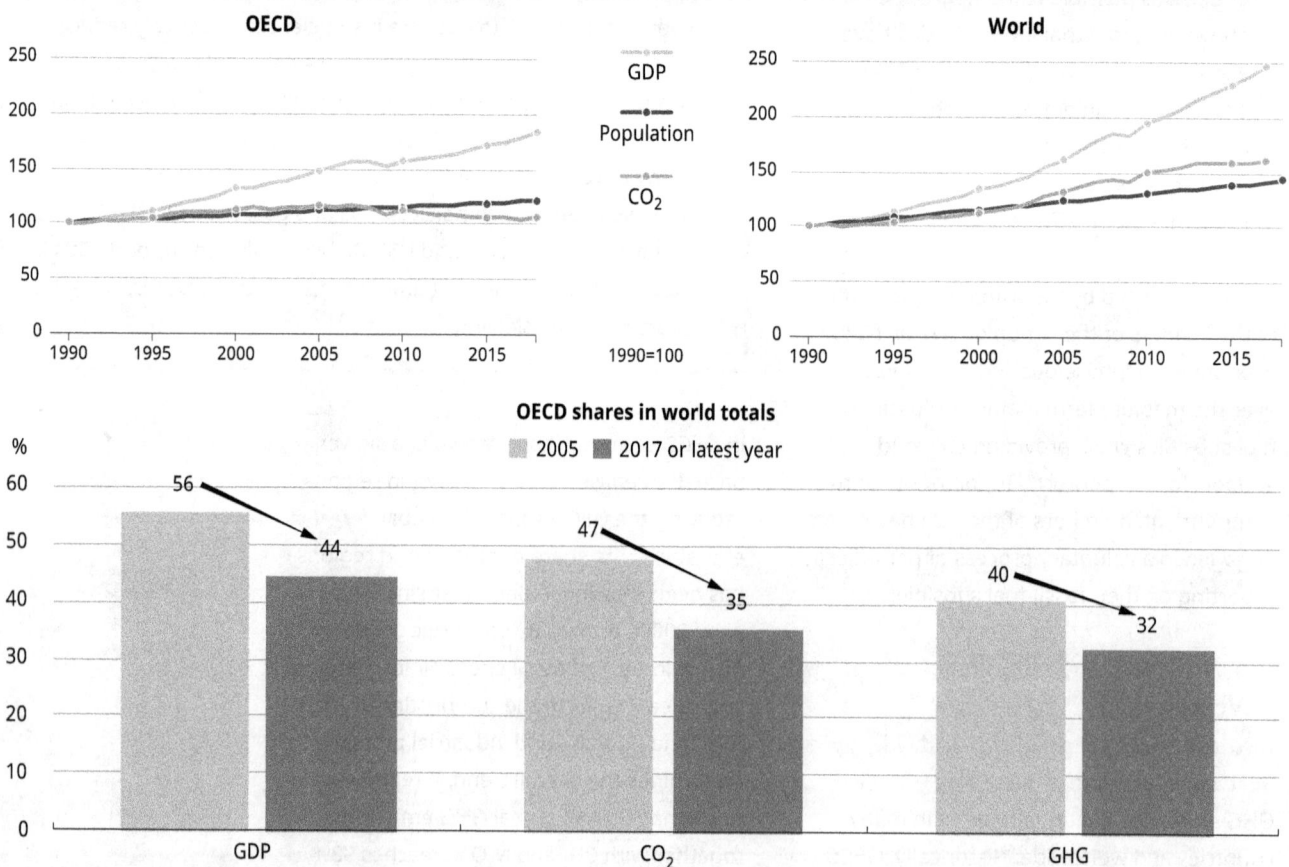

OECD

World

GDP

Population

CO_2

1990=100

OECD shares in world totals

2005   2017 or latest year

GDP: 56 → 44
CO_2: 47 → 35
GHG: 40 → 32

Source: IEA (2019), "Detailed CO_2 estimates", *IEA CO_2 Emissions from Fuel Combustion Statistics* (database); OECD (2019), "Aggregate National Accounts, SNA 2008 (or SNA 1993): Gross domestic product", *OECD National Accounts Statistics* (database); UN (2019), *UN World Population Prospects 2019*.

GHG emissions intensities, per unit of GDP

Kilograms of CO_2 equivalent per USD

2017 or latest year   2010   2000

GHG emissions intensities, per capita

Tonnes of CO_2 equivalent per capita

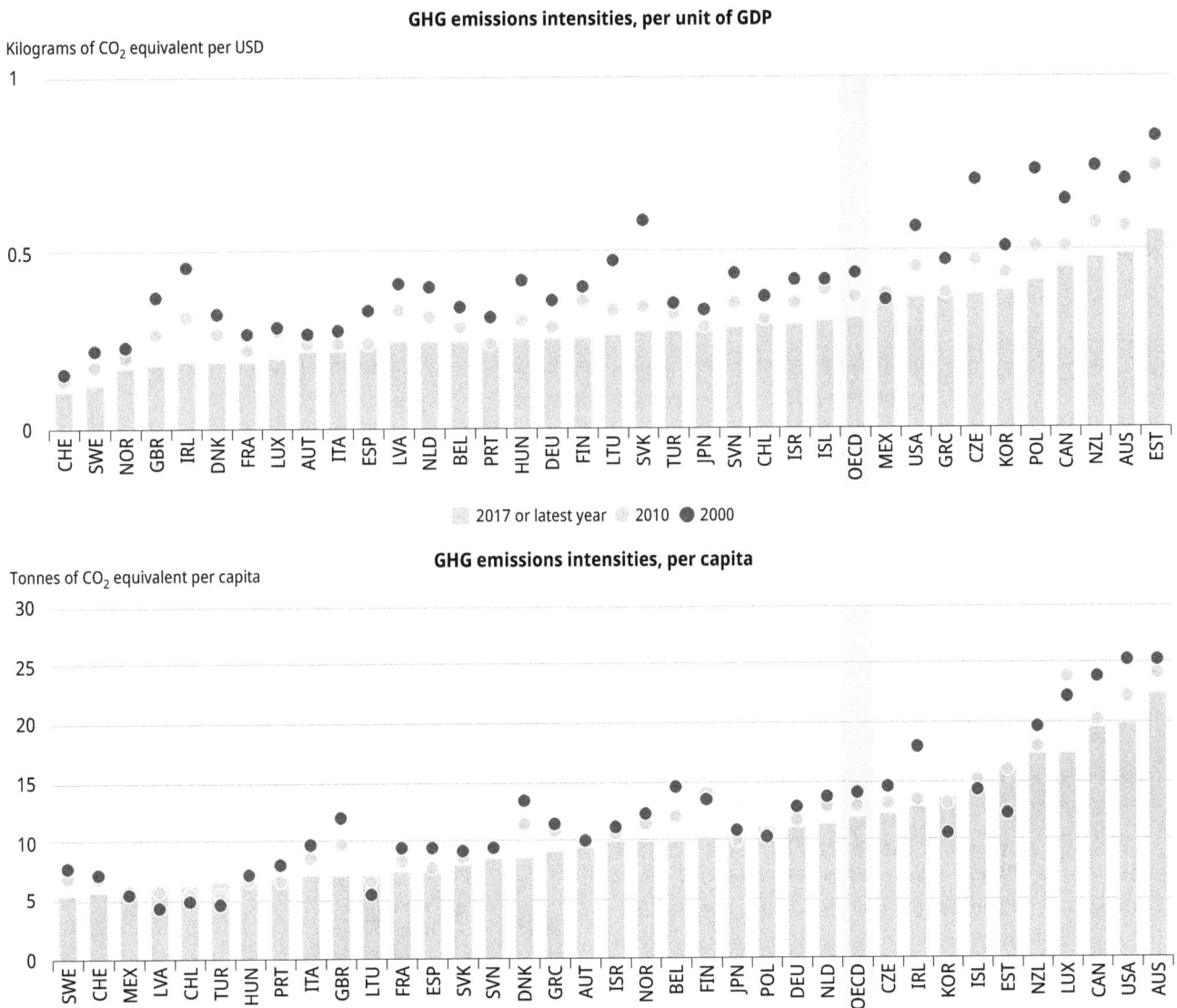

Note: The high per-GDP emissions of Estonia result from the use of oil shale for electricity generation (oil shale has a high carbon emission factor). The high per-capita emissions of Luxembourg result from a high number of cross-border workers and the lower taxation of road fuels compared to neighbouring countries, which attracts drivers to refuel in the country.

Source: OECD (2019), "Air and climate: Greenhouse gas emissions by source", *OECD Environment Statistics* (database).

Disaggregating GHG emissions shows substantial variations among sources and sectors. On average, electricity and heat generation contributes to 29% of the GHGs in OECD countries, followed by transport (24%), manufacturing industries (13%), agriculture, (9%), industrial processes (7%) and waste (2%). The share of emissions from electricity and heat generation and manufacturing decreased since 2005 thanks to gains in energy efficiency and cleaner technologies. The shares of transport and agriculture increased. In some countries transport accounts for more than 30% of total emissions (Luxembourg, Slovenia, Sweden, Switzerland); in other countries agriculture contributes to more than 30% (New Zealand, Ireland). Low-emission transitions are needed in all these sectors.

Energy-related CO_2 emissions of OECD countries have since 2000 grown at a slower rate than economic growth. This is due to structural changes in industry and energy supply and improvements in energy efficiency in production processes. Following the 2008 economic crisis emissions even decreased. Individual countries' rates of progress vary, regardless of whether emissions are considered in absolute numbers, per capita amounts or per unit of GDP. This is partly because of different national circumstances, such as the composition and rate of economic growth, socio-demographic developments, energy supply and consumption patterns, and energy prices, and partly because of policy measures taken to reduce emissions and to price carbon. Most countries achieved a relative decoupling between CO$_2$ emissions and economic growth over the past three decades; some managed to reduce emission levels in absolute terms. While decreasing in OECD America and OECD Europe, energy-related CO$_2$ emissions continue to grow in the OECD Asia-Oceania region.

Overall progress is insufficient

Progress in reducing GHG emissions is insufficient. Climate change is occurring faster than expected and increasingly impacts well-being, economic activities, biodiversity and ecosystems, including oceans.

Despite stronger climate policies and some progress in decoupling GHG emissions from economic growth in OECD countries, global emissions continue to grow, and 2018 data show that energy-related carbon emissions in the OECD area have risen again after 10 years of decline.

The carbon footprint of OECD countries that accounts for all carbon emitted anywhere in the world to satisfy domestic final demand is generally higher than domestic emissions (+18%). This is because OECD countries have

HOW DOES CLIMATE CHANGE AFFECT OCEANS?

The ocean absorbs over 25% of all anthropogenic GHG emissions from the atmosphere each year. The uptake of atmospheric CO$_2$ by the ocean changes the chemical composition of the seawater and causes ocean acidification. Over the past 30 years ocean acidity has increased by 26% on average compared to pre-industrial levels, and it could increase by 100% to 150% by the end of the century. Ocean acidification has the potential to change marine ecosystems and affect ocean-related benefits to society such as coastal protection or provision of food and income. It affects the formation and dissolution of calcium carbonate shells and skeletons in a range of marine species, including corals, molluscs such as oysters and mussels, and many phytoplankton and zooplankton species that form the base of marine food webs.

Ocean acidification is happening in parallel with other climate-related stressors, including ocean warming and deoxygenation. Interaction between these stressors (also referred to as the 'deadly trio') is often cumulative or even multiplicative. Increased ocean temperatures affect the physiology of marine organisms and influence the geographical distribution of species. Some species such as reef-forming corals, that already live at their upper

tolerance level, will have more difficulties 'moving' to new areas. Drastic changes in ocean temperature can also lead to coral bleaching. The role of coral reefs in buffering coastal communities from storm waves and erosion, and in supporting income generation for local communities and businesses through fisheries and tourism, is jeopardised. With continued ocean and atmospheric warming, sea levels will likely rise for many centuries at rates higher than that of the current century. The two major causes of global sea level rise are thermal expansion (water expands as it warms) and melting of ice, such as glaciers and ice sheets.

Sources: UNSD (2019),https://unstats.un.org/sdgs/report/2019/The-Sustainable-Development-Goals-Report-2019.pdf;
IUCN https://www.iucn.org/resources/issues-briefs/ocean-acidification

increasingly outsourced the production of consumer goods to other countries. Decoupling such demand-based emissions is challenging. The per capita footprint is highly correlated with material living standards, whereas per capita domestic emissions generally reflect the structure and energy intensity of the economy.

Levels of GHG concentrations in the atmosphere reached a record high in 2018, representing 147% (CO_2), 259% (CH_4) and 123% (N_2O) of pre-industrial levels (WMO, GHG bulletin 2018). Since 1990, there has been a 43% increase in total radiative forcing by long-lived GHG. CO_2 accounts for about 80% of this (US NOAA, 2019). This drives long-term climate change, sea level rise, ocean acidification and more extreme weather and related disasters. It is estimated that direct economic losses from climate-related disasters represented 77% of all disaster-related losses (USD 3 trillion) over the period 1998-2017, a rise of about 150% compared to the period 1978-97. Losses are disproportionately borne by vulnerable developing countries (UNSD 2019).

Energy production and use play a key role in GHG emissions

The main drivers behind GHG emissions in OECD countries are energy production and use, in particular fossil fuel use in the transport sector, in industry and by households.

In the 1990s and 2000s, energy intensity per unit of GDP decreased for OECD countries overall as a consequence of structural changes in the economy and energy conservation measures, and, since 2009, as a consequence of the slowdown in economic activity following the economic crisis. The overall decrease is 38% since 1990 and 23% since 2005. In some countries, the decrease was due to outsourcing of energy-intensive industrial production to other countries. Progress in per capita terms has been slower, reflecting an overall increase in total primary energy supply (TPES) between 1990 and 2018 and a growing energy demand for transport. TPES per capita has declined in about two thirds of OECD countries, and by about 3% on average in the OECD area since 1990 and 11% since 2005.

Figure 3. The energy intensity of OECD economies continues to improve, but progress is slow

Energy supply intensities, per unit of GDP

Tonnes of oil equivalent per thousand USD   2018   2010   ● 2000

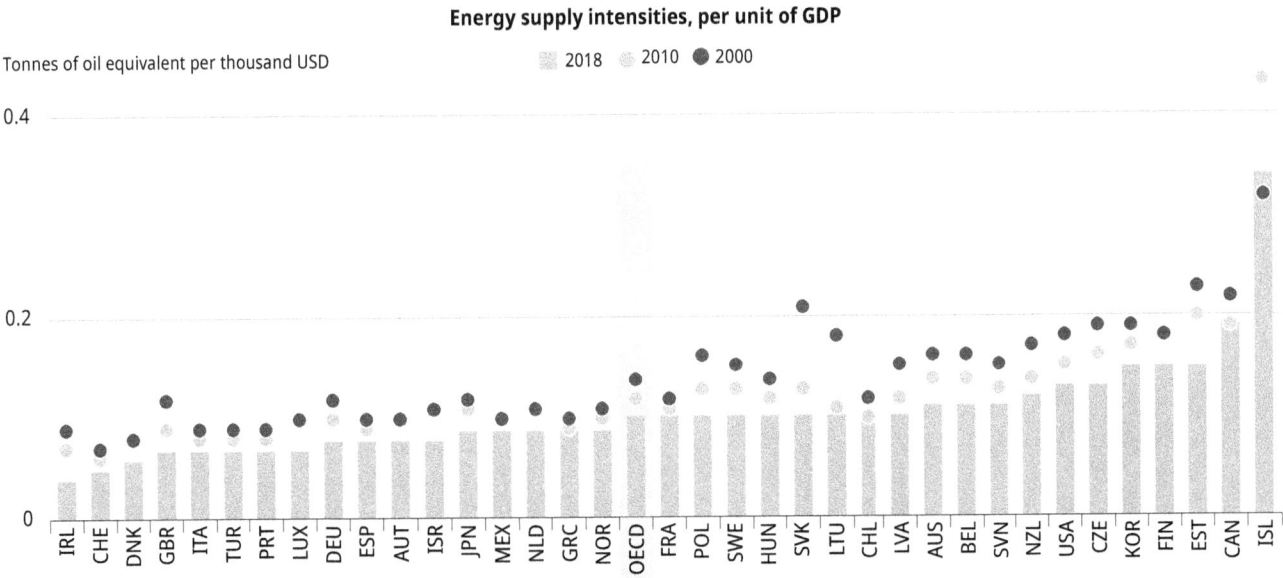

Note: The high value for Iceland is due to a significant increase in the production of hydro- and geothermal power mainly used in aluminium smelters.

Source: IEA (2019), "World energy statistics", IEA World Energy Statistics and Balances (database).

Variations in energy intensity among OECD countries are wide. They depend on national economic structure and income, geography, energy policies and prices, and countries' endowment in different types of energy resources. Relative decoupling between energy supply (TPES) and economic growth (GDP) is occurring in all regions of the OECD: since the 1990s in OECD Europe and OECD America; since the early 2000s in OECD Asia-Oceania. But results to date are insufficient to effectively reduce GHG emissions from energy use.

Fossil fuels dominate the energy mix and are subsidised

Developments in energy supply and intensity were accompanied by changes in the energy mix. Since 2000, OECD countries' reliance on fossil fuels has declined, but remains close to 80%. The shares of coal and oil fell slightly, while those of natural gas and renewable energy rose.

Renewables (i.e. solar, wind, liquid biofuels and biogases) exhibited the highest growth rates over the last decade. Their growth was less affected by the economic crisis and is driven by developments in OECD Europe, mostly due to the implementation of policies that promote the use of renewable energy. Europe's energy mix has the lowest share of fossil fuels among OECD regions (72%). Renewable energy sources however still represent a small share of energy use in OECD countries: 10% of TPES and 26% of electricity production on average. The largest renewable sources are biofuels and waste, followed by hydro.

Many governments continue to support fossil fuel production and use financially, in particular oil and gas. This undermines the effectiveness of environmental policies by lowering the cost of emitting carbon and is a barrier to moving towards a more energy-efficient and low-carbon economy. It can also impose a strain on government budgets.

In 2017, OECD countries provided around USD 80 billion of such support. This is 26% less than the highest amount in 2013. This decrease in support is in large part explained by reductions in general services support estimates (GSSE) and producer support estimates (PSE). In comparison, BRIICS countries (Brazil, Russian Federation, India, Indonesia, People's Republic of China, South Africa) provided around USD 47 billion of such support in 2017. This is 61% less than the highest amount in 2013. This decrease in support is in large part explained by reductions in consumer support estimates (CSE) and producer support estimates (PSE).

Most of the support in OECD countries (78%) goes to the consumption of fossil fuels, in particular oil. For several countries, estimates of support pertain exclusively to consumption, a feature that has much to do with geological factors and the decline in coal production observed throughout Europe. In countries possessing abundant fossil energy resources,

Figure 4. The share of renewables is growing, but remains too low

OECD primary energy mix

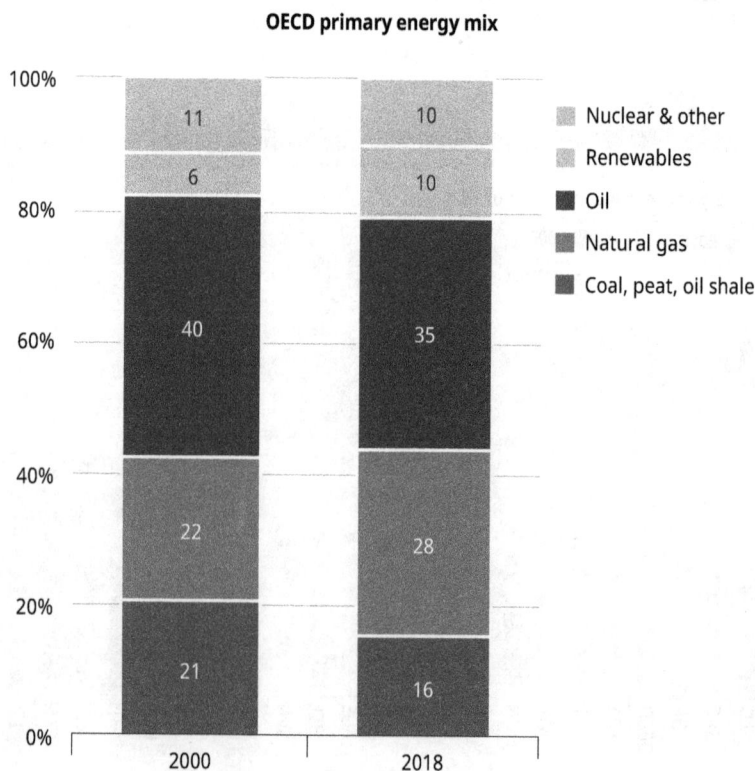

Legend:
- Nuclear & other
- Renewables
- Oil
- Natural gas
- Coal, peat, oil shale

	2000	2018
Nuclear & other	11	10
Renewables	6	10
Oil	40	35
Natural gas	22	28
Coal, peat, oil shale	21	16

Note: Data exclude electricity trade.

Source: IEA (2019), "World energy statistics", *IEA World Energy Statistics and Balances* (database).

the share of producer support tends to be higher. On the production side, the subsidised hard-coal industry in several EU countries has been phased out and efforts to end state aid to coal-fired power generation in the European Union are continuing. A recent EU decision aims at ending state aid to high-emission power plants by 2025. At the same time, the oil and gas sector continues to benefit from government incentives in several countries, mostly through tax provisions that provide preferential treatment for cost recovery. Such policies could go against domestic efforts to reduce global GHG emissions.

BOX 1. A CLOSER LOOK AT BLACK CARBON

Several gases have direct effects on climate change: carbon dioxide (CO_2), methane (CH_4), nitrous oxide (N_2O), chlorofluorocarbons (CFCs), hydrofluorocarbons (HCFCs), perfluorocarbons (PFCs) and sulphur hexafluoride (SF_6). Local air pollutants also play a direct or indirect role. Black carbon, a component of fine particulate matter (PM2.5) for example has direct effects on climate. Pollutants such as non-methane volatile organic compounds (NMVOC), nitrogen oxides (NOx) and carbon monoxide (CO), have *indirect effects* as their reactions in the atmosphere result in the production of tropospheric ozone (O_3) – a greenhouse gas (GHG). Sulphur containing trace gases also play a role.

Carbon dioxide is the main anthropogenic greenhouse gas (GHG). It remains in the atmosphere for several years or decades. Other gases and substances, such as CH_4, O_3 and black carbon, have shorter atmospheric residence times, from a few days to a decade. These short-lived climate forcers (SLCFs) have a relatively stronger warming impact in the short run. Reducing their emissions can thus have immediate effects on atmospheric warming, while at the same time improving air quality with benefits for human health, agricultural production and ecosystems.

Black carbon (BC) raises concerns because of its impacts on human health and the environment. It causes respiratory and vascular diseases, and accelerates global warming. Due to its dark colour, BC is the most light-absorbing part of PM2.5 and has a high radiative forcing. It traps 680 times more heat than CO_2, making it a major contributor to atmospheric warming.

Black carbon results from the incomplete combustion of fossil fuels, in particular diesel, kerosene, biofuels and biomass. The main sources are residential and commercial, followed by transport. Other important sources are forest fires and agricultural burning. In the atmosphere, BC remains suspended for days to weeks before it deposits on the ground. It is often more concentrated near emission sources, but it can also travel vast distances in the air and reach remote areas.

Black carbon pollution is particularly worrying in the Arctic region that increasingly faces concentration peaks. It plays an important role in the Arctic radiation budget and accelerates ice melting. The Arctic is warming at twice the global average rate, with repercussions at the global level.

Reaching the 1.5°C climate goal of the Paris Agreement will require reductions in emissions of both major GHG and SLCFs. Research has shown that global warming could be abated by 0.5 Celsius degrees by 2050 if SLCFs emissions are reduced. Member countries of the Arctic Council, except the United States, have committed to take collective action to reduce their aggregate BC emissions by 25-33% by 2025 compared to 2013 levels.

Sources:
Arctic Council (2019), "Expert Group on Black Carbon and Methane – Summary of Progress and Recommendations 2019", Arctic Council; Secretariat, Tromsø, https://oaarchive.arctic-council.org/handle/11374/2411; United States Climate Alliance, http://www.usclimatealliance.org/slcpchallenge; Climate and Clean Air Coalition, https://www.ccacoalition.org/ru/slcps/black-carbon.

2 AIR QUALITY AND HEALTH

Air pollution is the world's leading environmental health risk and a major cause of environmental degradation. It can have substantial economic and social consequences, from health costs and reduced labour productivity to forest damage and reduced agricultural output. The main contributors to air pollution are atmospheric pollutants from energy transformation and use, and industrial processes.

Progress is measured through indicators on emissions of air pollutants (SO_x, NO_x, PM2.5), human exposure to fine particulates in the air and related mortality rates and costs.

Industry is a major contributor to poor air quality
Photo © M. Shcherbyna/Shutterstock.com

THE ISSUE

Air pollution is the world's leading environmental health risk and a major cause of environmental degradation, threatening many ecosystems. Degraded air quality can have substantial economic and social consequences, from health costs, reduced labour productivity and a lower quality of life to infrastructure maintenance, reduced agricultural output and forest damage. Human exposure is particularly high in urban areas where economic activities are concentrated and where demand for mobility is highest. Some population groups are especially vulnerable to air pollution. The very young and the very old are the most at risk.

The main contributors to regional and local air pollution are atmospheric pollutants from energy transformation, energy consumption and industrial processes, including sulphur oxides (SOx), nitrogen oxides (NO_x), ozone (O_3), non-methane volatile organic compounds (NMVOC) and particulate matter.

- Sulphur and nitrogen oxides are transformed into acidifying substances such as sulphuric and nitric acid in the atmosphere. When these substances reach the ground, acidification of soil, water and buildings occurs which causes severe environmental damage. Nitrogen oxides also contribute to the formation of ground-level ozone that is effectively a greenhouse gas, and are responsible for eutrophication, reduction in water quality and species richness. High concentrations cause respiratory diseases.

- Fine particulate matter (PM2.5), is of particular concern from a human health perspective. Chronic exposure even to moderate levels of PM2.5 increases the risk of heart disease and stroke, the leading causes of death in OECD countries. It also increases the risk of respiratory diseases, including lung cancer, chronic obstructive pulmonary disease and

The main contributors to regional and local air pollution are atmospheric pollutants from energy transformation, energy consumption and industrial processes.

respiratory infections. Black carbon, a major component of fine particulate matter, accelerates global warming and fosters snowmelt.

POLICY CHALLENGES

The main challenges are to further reduce emissions of local and regional air pollutants, to achieve a strong decoupling of emissions from economic growth and limit people's exposure to polluted air. This implies implementing effective pollution prevention and control policies and sustainable transport and mobility policies, stimulating investment in cleaner technologies and promoting energy efficiency and the substitution of dirty fuels with cleaner ones. Behavioural and lifestyle changes are also important, as well as spatial planning.

Since sources of air pollution and severity of exposure vary across and within countries, it is important to tailor policies to specific local circumstances. More stringent measures may for example be required in densely populated areas or for emission sources located upwind from urban areas. Policies that provide incentives across a broad spectrum of firms and consumers, such as emission or energy taxes, tend to be more cost-efficient than those that target a specific product, fuel or technology, such as financial support for low or zero emission vehicles.

MEASURING PERFORMANCE AND PROGRESS

Environmental performance can be evaluated against domestic objectives and international goals and commitments.

Reducing negative impacts of degraded air quality is part of the 2030 Agenda for Sustainable Development (New York, September 2015) under Goal 3 *"Ensure healthy lives and promote well-being for all at all ages"* and under Goal 11 *"Make cities and human settlements inclusive, safe, resilient and sustainable"*

BOX 2. HOW DOES AIR POLLUTION AFFECT HUMAN HEALTH?

Adverse effects on human health can occur as a result of short- or long-term exposure to air pollution. The pollutants with the strongest evidence of health effects are particulate matter (PM), ozone (O_3), nitrogen dioxide (NO_2) and sulphur dioxide (SO_2).

Particulate matter (PM) consists of a complex mixture of solid and liquid particles of organic and inorganic substances suspended in the air. Major components are sulfates, nitrates, ammonia, sodium chloride, black carbon, mineral dust and water. Particulates are emitted by combustion processes (motor vehicles, industrial combustion, residential heating), and industrial processes and activities such as construction, mining, cement manufacture and smelting. Particulates are also formed in the atmosphere through chemical reaction of precursor pollutants, mainly nitrogen oxides, sulphur dioxide and ammoniac. There is a close, quantitative relationship between exposure to high concentrations of particulates and increased mortality or morbidity, both daily and over time. Small particulates of less than 10 μm in diameter (PM10) are capable of penetrating deep into the respiratory tract and causing significant health damage. Chronic exposure to particles contributes to the risk of developing cardiovascular and respiratory diseases, as well as lung cancer. Fine particulates smaller than 2.5 microns in diameter (PM2.5) cause even more severe health effects because they penetrate deeper into the respiratory tract and because they are potentially more toxic and may include heavy metals and toxic organic substances.

Ozone at ground level – not to be confused with the ozone layer in the upper atmosphere – is one of the major constituents of photochemical smog. It is not directly emitted, but formed by the reaction with sunlight (photochemical reaction) of pollutants such as nitrogen oxides, carbon monoxide (CO) and volatile organic compounds (VOCs). As a result, the highest levels of ozone pollution occur during periods of sunny weather. Excessive ozone in the air can have a marked effect on human health. It can cause breathing problems, trigger asthma, reduce lung function and cause respiratory diseases.

Nitrogen dioxide is emitted by road traffic, power generation and combustion in industry; it contributes to the formation of particulate matter and ozone. NO_2 can increase respiratory problems such as bronchitis and asthma, and lead to respiratory infections and reduced lung function and growth.

Sulphur dioxide is emitted from the burning of fossil fuels (coal, oil) and the smelting of mineral ores that contain sulphur. SO_2 affects the respiratory system and lung function, and causes eye irritation. It can aggravate bronchitis and asthma.

Source: based on WHO, https://www.who.int/ airpollution/ambient/en/.

In Europe and North America, acidification has led to several international agreements among which the Convention on Long-Range Transboundary Air Pollution (1979), and its eight protocols to reduce emissions of sulphur (Helsinki 1985, Oslo 1994, Gothenburg 1999), nitrogen oxides (Sofia 1988, Gothenburg 1999), volatile organic compounds (Geneva 1991, Gothenburg 1999), and ammonia (Gothenburg 1999). Two other protocols aim at reducing emissions of heavy metals (Aarhus 1998) and persistent organic pollutants (Aarhus 1998). The 2012 amendment of the Gothenburg protocol establishes legally binding emissions reduction commitments for 2020 and beyond for the major air pollutants: sulphur dioxide (SO_2), nitrogen oxides (NO_x), ammonia (NH_3), volatile organic compounds (VOCs) and fine particulate matter (PM2.5). It specifically includes the short-lived climate pollutant black carbon (or soot) as a component of particular matter. Reducing particulate matter through the implementation of the Protocol is thus a major step in reducing air pollution, while at the same time facilitating climate co-benefits.

MAIN TRENDS AND RECENT DEVELOPMENTS

Emissions of major air pollutants are decreasing in many OECD countries

Compared to 2000, SO_x and NO_x emissions continue to decrease for the OECD as a whole, and almost all OECD countries have achieved a strong decoupling from economic growth. These reductions are the combined result of changes in energy demand, energy savings and fuel substitution, pollution control policies and technical progress. In the late 2000s, the slowdown in economic activity following the 2008 economic crisis further contributed to mitigate emissions.

NO_x emissions decreased however at a slower pace than SO_x emissions, and their reduction has not compensated in all countries for the steady growth in road traffic, fossil fuel use and other activities generating NO_x. Several countries parties to the Gothenburg Protocol attained the NO_x emission ceilings for 2010; other countries had difficulties in doing so. All countries reached the SO_x emission ceilings for 2010. By 2017, almost all OECD countries reached their SO_x and NO_x emission targets for 2020; a few are on track to meet them. Emission intensities per capita and per unit of GDP show significant variations among OECD countries.

PM2.5 emission levels and intensities are decreasing in most OECD countries. This can be attributed to optimised combustion processes (in industry and in residential heating), a decrease of coal in the energy mix, and lower emissions from transport and agriculture. In some countries, such as Canada or the United States, emission levels and intensities remain high due to large construction sites, unpaved roads, fields, smokestacks or fire. On top of direct emissions, fine particulates also form in the atmosphere as a result of chemical reactions among precursor pollutants such as SO_x and NO_x.

┌─ **KEY MESSAGES ON AIR QUALITY AND HEALTH** ─────────

- SO_x and NO_x emissions continue to decrease in the OECD area, and almost all OECD countries have achieved a strong decoupling from economic growth since 2000. Reductions in NO_x emissions have however not compensated in all countries for the steady growth in road traffic, fossil fuel use and other activities generating NO_x.

- Emissions of fine particulates (PM2.5) and related intensities are decreasing in most OECD countries, thanks to optimised combustion processes, a decline of coal in the energy mix, and lower emissions from transport and agriculture.

- Mean exposure to PM2.5 has decreased in all OECD countries, but remains high. In two out of three countries inhabitants continue to be exposed to levels above the WHO guideline value of 10 µg/m³.

- Worldwide, premature deaths associated with PM2.5 pollution have increased, whereas they dropped in the OECD area. Central and Eastern European countries are the most affected with more than 500 estimated deaths per million inhabitants. The related welfare costs represent on average about 3% of GDP equivalent in the OECD area, compared to about 4% worldwide.

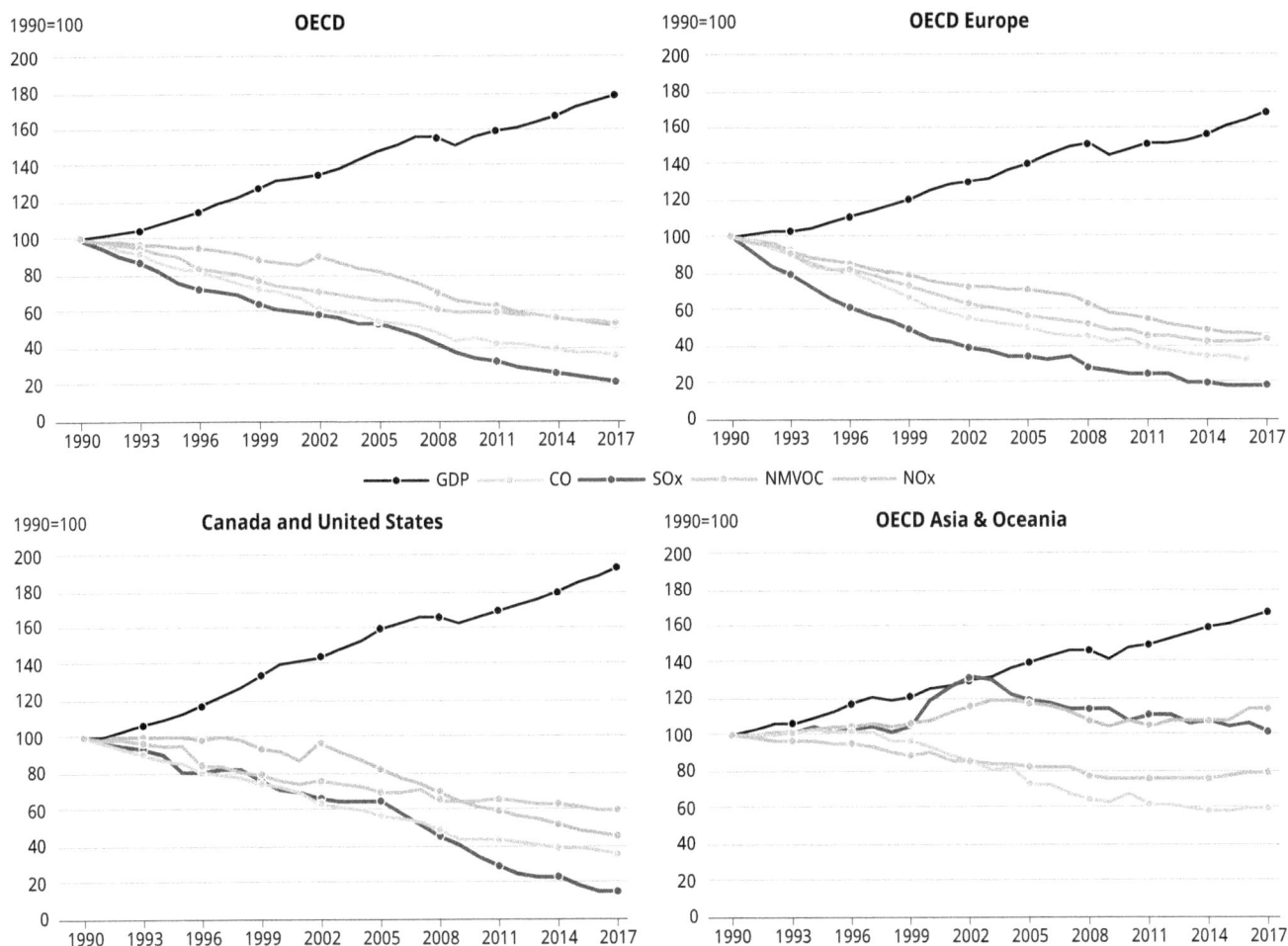

1990=100 **OECD**

1990=100 **OECD Europe**

Legend: GDP — CO — SOx — NMVOC — NOx

1990=100 **Canada and United States**

1990=100 **OECD Asia & Oceania**

Source: OECD (2019), "Air and climate: Air emissions by source", *OECD Environment Statistics* (database).

Air quality is improving in OECD countries, but human exposure remains too high

The decreasing emission trends led to improved air quality and reduced human exposure to air pollution in many cities. Mean population exposure to fine particulate matter (PM2.5) has decreased in all OECD countries, but remains high. In two out of three OECD countries, inhabitants are still exposed to levels exceeding the World Health Organization (WHO) air quality guideline value of 10µg of PM2.5/m³. Pollution by nitrogen dioxide also persists in many cities, in particular in areas where road traffic is dense.

Premature deaths due to PM2.5 pollution and welfare costs have decreased in almost all OECD countries, while they increased worldwide. In the OECD area, The welfare costs of premature deaths associated with PM2.5 pollution represent on average about 3% of GDP equivalent, compared to a global average of about 4%. Premature deaths and welfare costs are higher in Europe than in other OECD regions. Central and Eastern European countries are the most affected (Czech Republic, Hungary, Lithuania, Latvia, Poland, Slovak Republic), with more than 500 estimated deaths per million inhabitants.

Worldwide, population exposure to air pollution has on average recently stabilised but remains severe in low- and middle-income countries in Asia, the Middle East and Africa. In developing countries, exposure to pollutants also comes from indoor combustion of solid fuels in open fires or traditional stoves. It is estimated that in 2016, 9 in 10 people living in urban areas

NO$_x$ emissions intensities, per capita

Kilogram per capita

Country axis (left to right): CHE, TUR, CHL, JPN, ITA, SVK, HUN, FRA, SWE, GBR, ISR, NLD, DEU, BEL, CZE, MEX, ESP, AUT, PRT, SVN, LTU, LVA, DNK, POL, OECD, FIN, IRL, KOR, EST, GRC, USA, NOR, LUX, NZL, CAN, ISL, AUS

Legend: ▪ 2017 or latest year · 2010 ● 2000

PM2.5 emissions intensities, per capita

Kilogram per capita

Country axis (left to right): CHE, NLD, DEU, GBR, KOR, AUT, BEL, SWE, ESP, LUX, IRL, FRA, GRC, ITA, LTU, FIN, SVK, DNK, CZE, ISL, POL, TUR, PRT, MEX, HUN, NOR, SVN, EST, CHL, LVA, USA, CAN

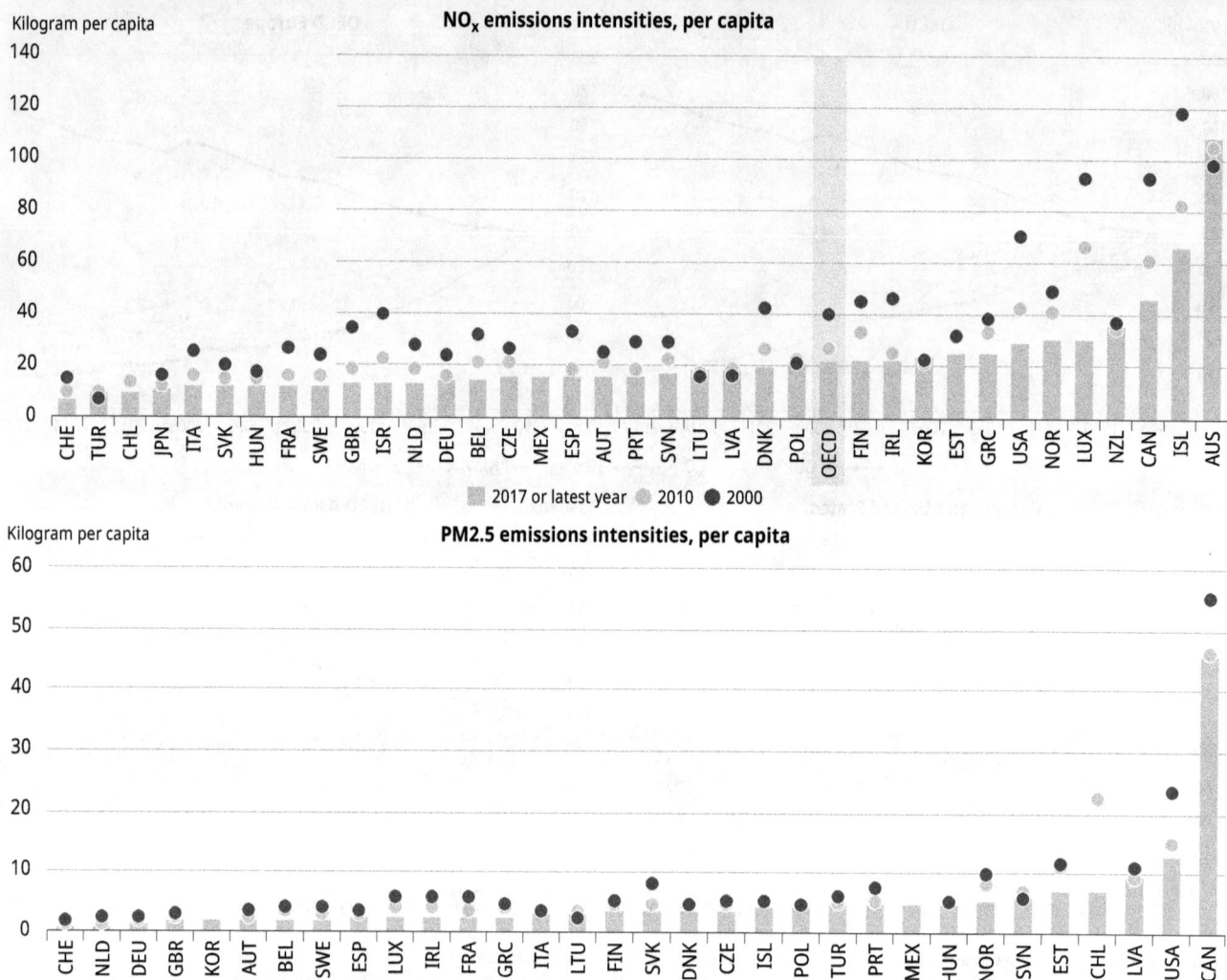

Note: High levels and rise of NO$_x$ emissions in Australia are due to industrial combustion, power stations and growing vehicle ownership. The high emission levels of PM2.5 for Canada is due to dust from construction operations and unpaved and paved roads.

Source: OECD (2019), "Air and climate: Air emissions by source", *OECD Environment Statistics* (database).

that monitor air pollution breathed air that exceeds the WHO guideline value for PM2.5. (WHO). Ambient air pollution in both cities and rural areas was estimated to have caused 4.2 million premature deaths worldwide in 2016. In combination with indoor air pollution, it caused about seven million premature deaths, largely as a result of increased mortality from stroke, heart disease, chronic pulmonary disease, lung cancer and acute respiratory infections.

It should be noted that exposure indicators provide only a partial and aggregated view of the consequences of air pollution, and that there is generally no "safe level" of exposure to many pollutants. Even when standards or guidelines are met, substantial public health and economic benefits can be realised through further improvements in air quality. Reducing road traffic, urban congestion and motor vehicle emissions could have a great impact on NO$_2$ and particulate concentrations. It can be achieved through shifts in transport modes, electrification of vehicle fleets, promotion of active mobility (walking, cycling) and public transport, and a proper integration of air quality and mobility policies in spatial planning. In countries where the use of biomass (wood) for residential heating is common, measures to prevent and control PM2.5 emissions from fire places and stoves are also needed.

Mean population exposure to fine particulates (PM2.5), 2017

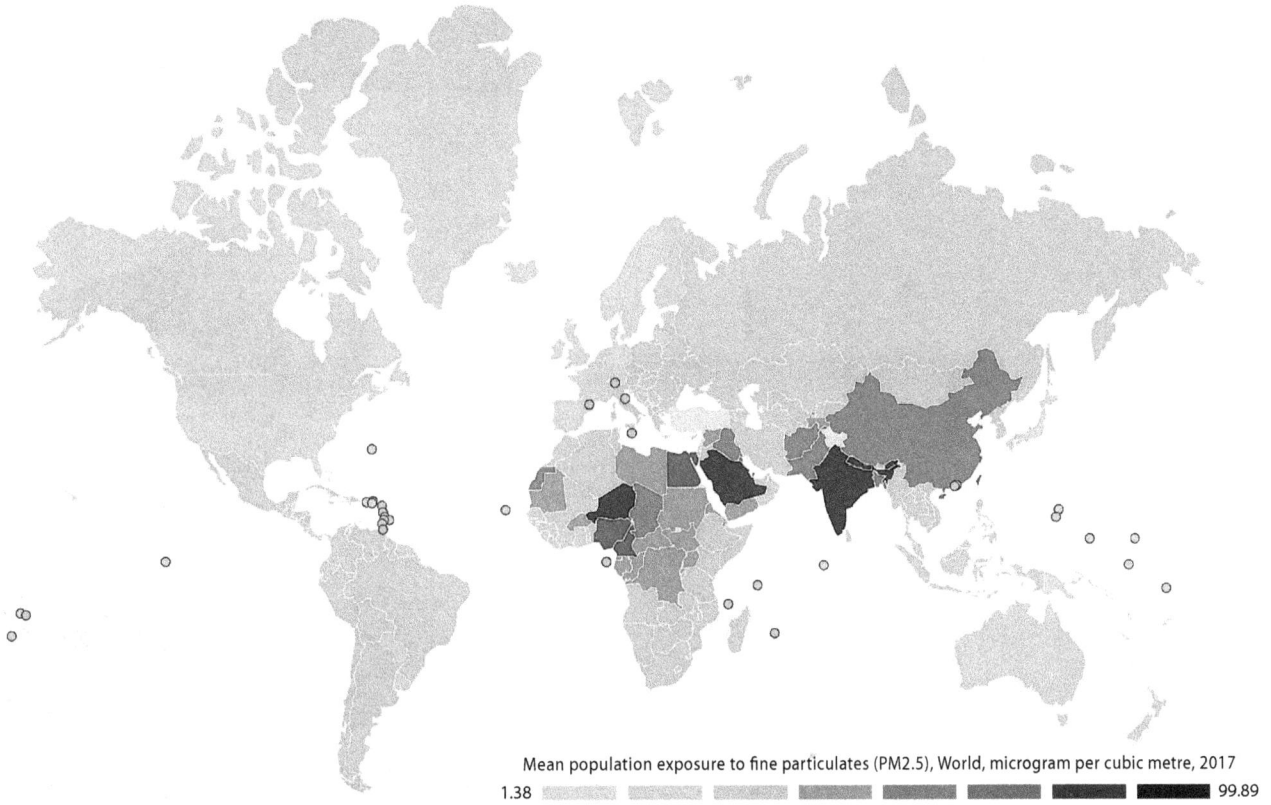

Mean population exposure to fine particulates (PM2.5), World, microgram per cubic metre, 2017
1.38 ▭▭▭▭▭▭▭▭ 99.89

Mean population exposure to fine particulates (PM2.5), 2000

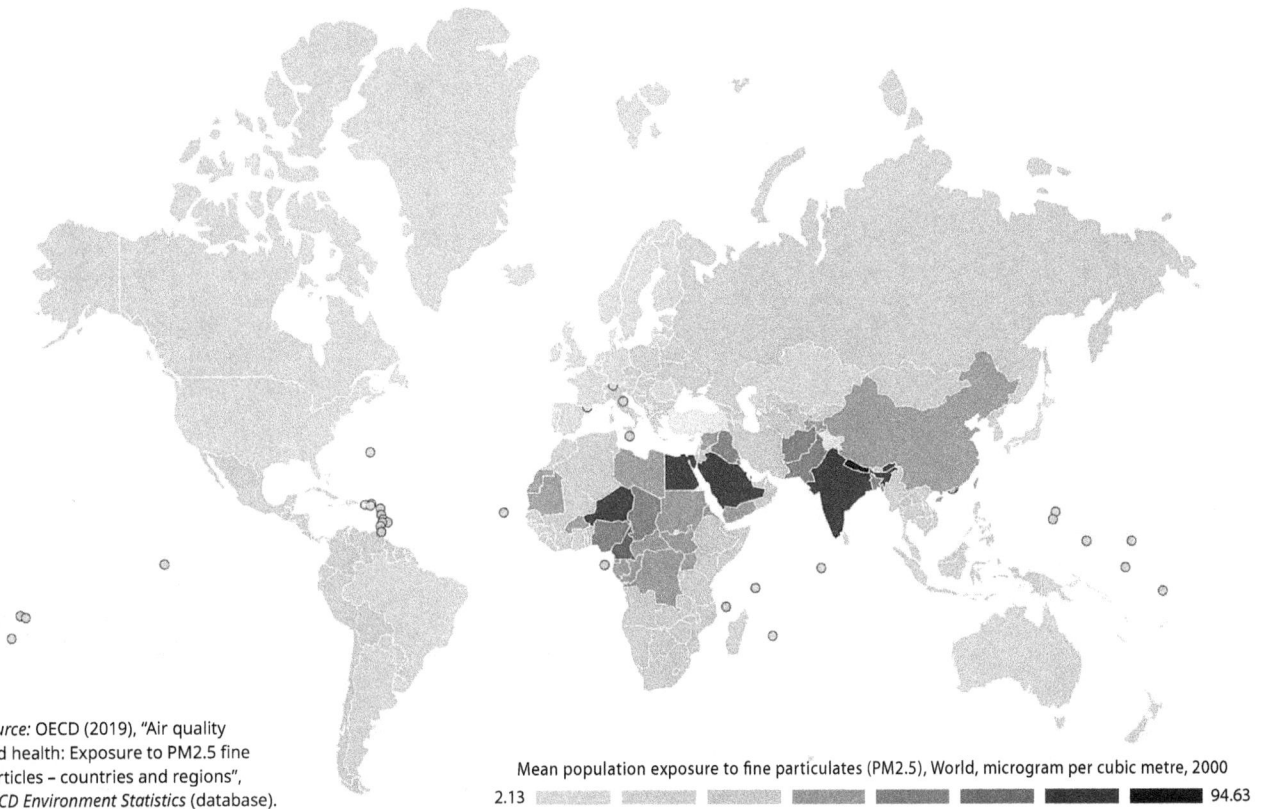

Source: OECD (2019), "Air quality and health: Exposure to PM2.5 fine particles – countries and regions", *OECD Environment Statistics* (database).

Mean population exposure to fine particulates (PM2.5), World, microgram per cubic metre, 2000
2.13 ▭▭▭▭▭▭▭▭ 94.63

3 FRESHWATER RESOURCES

Freshwater resources are of major environmental, economic and social importance. Overexploitation, inefficient use and changes in climate and weather conditions can lead to low river flows, depleted groundwater and degraded water quality, loss of wetlands, desertification and risks for food security and economic production. Ensuring sustainable management of water resources is key to maintaining adequate supplies of freshwater for human use and to support aquatic and other ecosystems.

Progress is measured through indicators on freshwater abstractions, water stress levels, and connection rates to wastewater treatment plants.

Derwent reservoir, United Kingdom
Photo © MichaelWalkerUK/Shutterstock.com

THE ISSUE

Freshwater resources are of major environmental, economic and social importance. They are unevenly distributed among and within countries. If a significant share of a country's water comes from transboundary rivers, tensions between countries can arise. In arid regions, freshwater resources may, at times, be limited to the extent that demand for water can be met only by going beyond sustainable use.

Abstractions for public supply of drinking water, irrigation, industrial processes and cooling of electric power plants, exert major pressure on freshwater resources, with significant implications for their quantity and quality. Other factors that play a role are changes in climate and weather conditions, pollution loads from human activities (agriculture, industry, households), and infrastructure developments that affect the natural integrity of rivers, lakes, aquifers and wetlands. Overexploitation and inefficient use can lead to low river flows, depleted groundwater and degraded water quality, loss of wetlands, desertification and risks for food security and economic production. If pressure from human activities becomes so intense that water quality is impaired to the point that it requires ever more advanced treatment, or that aquatic plant and animals in rivers and lakes are threatened, then the sustainability of water resource use is in question.

POLICY CHALLENGES

The main challenge is to ensure sustainable management of water resources and water services to maintain adequate supplies of freshwater of suitable quality for economic activities, human use and well-being, support aquatic and other ecosystems, and address threats associated with droughts and floods resulting from climate change. This requires an integrated approach for the management of water and water-related ecosystems and an effective cooperation in transboundary river basins.

Abstractions for public supply of drinking water, irrigation, industrial processes and cooling of electric power plants, exert major pressure on freshwater resources, with significant implications for their quantity and quality.

- Water quantity is best managed through a combination of policies that manage demand for water, promote water use efficiency, and allocate water where it is most needed.

- Water quality management requires preventing and reducing pollution from all sources, through a systematic integration of water quality considerations in agricultural and other policies and appropriate treatment of wastewater. Both polluters and users should be kept accountable.

- Water risks and disasters are best managed in a cooperative way through risk assessments and a mix of prevention and mitigation measures. Policy coherence across climate change adaptation, water management, land management, spatial planning, biodiversity protection and disaster risk reduction is crucial.

Policy instruments such as pricing of water and water-related services are important for managing demand and promoting efficient use of water, for allocating water among competing uses and for generating finance to invest in water-related infrastructure and services. At the same time, the affordability of the water bill for low income households needs to be taken into account to ensure continued access to water for poorer consumers. Water pricing can be complemented by a range of other instruments and measures, including abstraction and pollution charges, tradable water permits, smart metering, water reuse and innovation.

MEASURING PERFORMANCE AND PROGRESS

Environmental performance can be assessed against domestic objectives and international goals and commitments.

Preservation of water resources and management of wastewater are part of the 2030 Agenda for Sustainable Development

(New York, September 2015) under Goal 6 *"Ensure availability and sustainable management of water and sanitation for all"*, and Goal 3 *"Ensure healthy lives and promote well-being for all at all ages"*.

Main international agreements and legislation include the OSPAR Convention on the Protection of the North-East Atlantic Marine Environment, the International Joint Commission Agreement on Great Lakes Water Quality in North America and the EU water directives. At national level countries have set receiving water standards, effluent limits, pollution load reduction targets and established water permits.

MAIN TRENDS AND RECENT DEVELOPMENTS

Pressures on freshwater resources continue to grow, but abstractions have been decoupled from economic growth in many OECD countries

Pressures on water resources continue to mount, and competition for access to water is increasing driven by economic and population growth. At global level, freshwater abstractions continue to grow at a faster rate than the population.

In the OECD area, freshwater abstractions have on average decoupled from economic and population growth, with per capita abstractions declining since 2000. Results

┌─ KEY MESSAGES ON FRESHWATER RESOURCES ─

- Pressures on freshwater resources continue to mount, and competition for access to water is increasing driven by economic and population growth. Global abstractions continue to grow at a faster rate than population growth, with agriculture using about 70% of all abstractions.

- In the OECD area, freshwater abstractions have decoupled from economic and population growth, with average per capita abstractions declining since 2000. In many countries, the volumes of freshwater used for irrigation has declined.

- The average level of water stress has diminished in most OECD countries since 2000 thanks to improvements in technologies and resource management. Very few countries experience medium-to-high water stress, but most face seasonal or local water quantity problems that can constrain economic development and human well-being.

- The provision of wastewater treatment services has improved in the OECD area since 2000. In more than one third of the countries over 80% of the population are connected to a sewage treatment plant with at least secondary treatment. Challenges remain as regards the upgrading of existing treatment infrastructure, and servicing small and isolated settlements with adequate treatment systems.

vary within and among countries, but the information available to assess countries' water resources remains insufficient to carry out a more thorough analysis. The highest per capita abstractions are found in the OECD America region, at above 1 000 m³/inhabitant mainly driven by the United States, followed

Freshwater public supply per capita

■ 2017 or latest   ● 2000

m³/capita

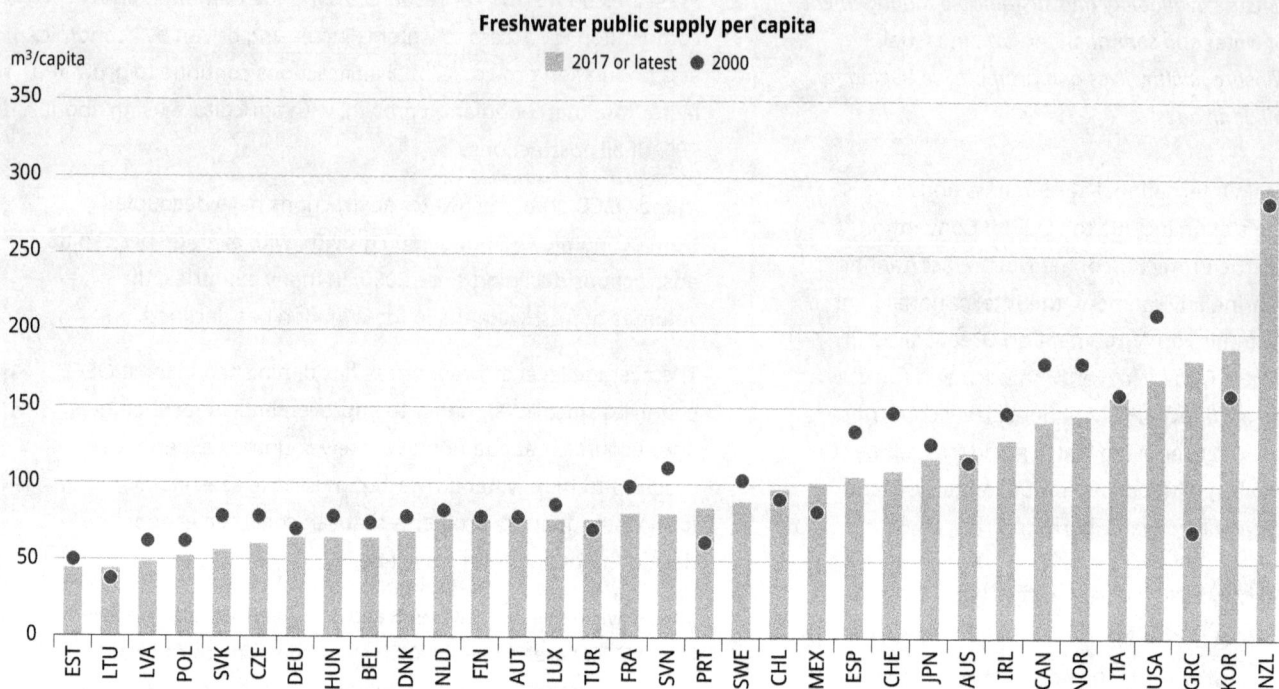

Source: OECD (2019), "Water: Freshwater abstractions", *OECD Environment Statistics* (database).

The share of abstracted freshwater used for irrigation ranges from close to zero in Iceland to over 70% in Greece and Turkey.

by the OECD Asia-Oceania region (around 620 m³/inhabitant) and the OECD Europe region (around 480 m³/inhabitant). The uses for which freshwater is abstracted vary across countries. Some countries devote over half of their abstractions to public supply of drinking water, others allocate it mostly to agriculture (e.g. Turkey, Mexico, Spain, Greece) or to electrical cooling (e.g. Germany, France). Per capita abstractions for public supply have generally decreased in the OECD area.

Worldwide, agriculture uses about 70% of all abstractions, mainly for irrigation and livestock. In the OECD area, the share of irrigation in total abstractions varies greatly across countries depending on the structure of their economy, climatic conditions and agricultural practices that influence irrigation needs. The share of abstracted freshwater used for irrigation ranges from close to zero in Iceland to over 70% in Greece and Turkey. In many countries, the use of freshwater for irrigation has been declining since 2000, albeit at varying rates. In some countries, it recently increased again (e.g. Canada, Korea).

Average water stress levels have diminished, but vary greatly within and among countries

As of the 1980s, some countries have been stabilising their abstractions thanks to more efficient irrigation techniques, the decline of water-intensive industries, increased use of more efficient technologies and reduced losses in pipe networks. In some cases stabilisation was achieved by using alternative water sources, including water reuse and desalination. As a result the average level of water stress has been diminishing in most OECD countries over the past decades. Very few countries experience medium-to-high water stress. National water stress levels however hide important variations at subnational (e.g. river basin) level. Some countries have extensive arid and semi-arid regions, and most countries face seasonal or local water quantity problems that can constrain economic development and human well-being. It is estimated that globally, about one third of countries have medium or high levels of water stress, most countries with high water stress being located in North Africa, West Asia or in Central and South Asia.

Freshwater stress, 2017 or latest year available

%   ▨ as % of renewable resources   ▨ as % of internal resources

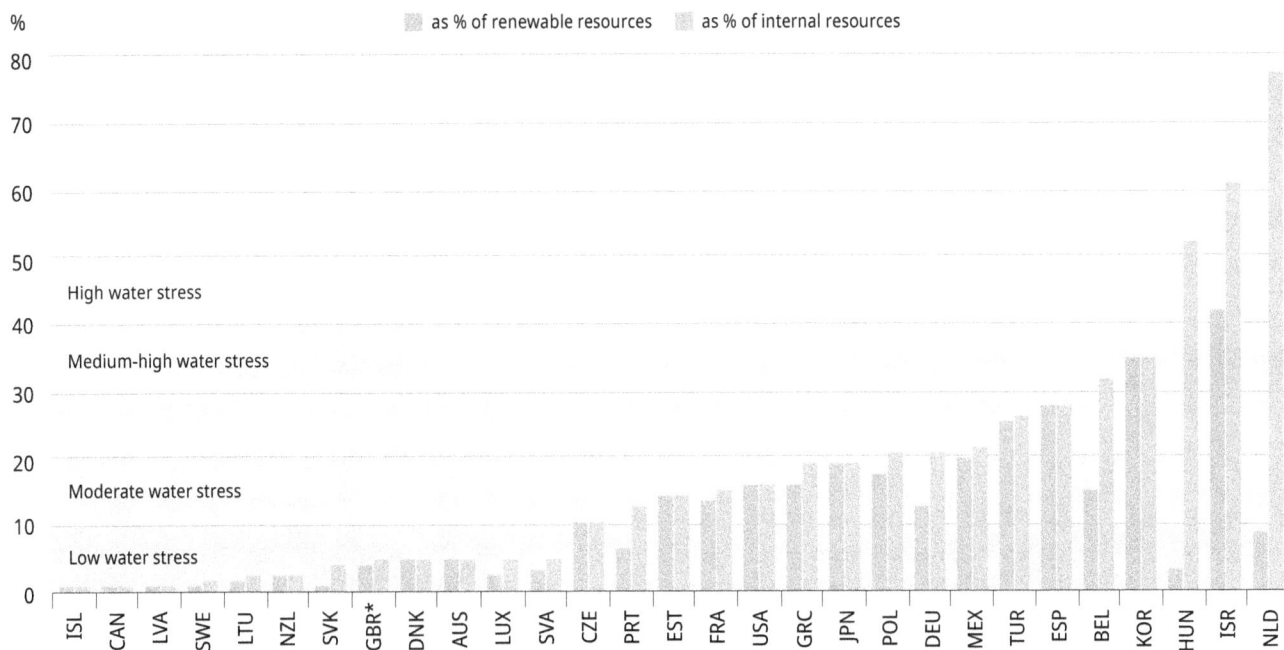

Note: The following stress levels can be distinguished:

Low (less than 10%): generally there is no major stress on the available resources.

Moderate (10% to 20%): indicates that water availability issues are becoming a constraint on development and significant investments are needed to provide adequate supplies.

Medium-high (20% to 40%): implies the management of both supply and demand, and conflicts among competing uses need to be resolved.

High (more than 40%): indicates serious scarcity, and usually shows unsustainable water use, which can become a limiting factor in social and economic development.

*England & Wales only

Source: OECD (2019), "Water: Freshwater abstractions", *OECD Environment Statistics* (database).

Most people in OECD countries benefit from public sewage treatment, but challenges remain regarding the maintenance of infrastructure and the treatment of emerging pollutants

Progress at global level with sewage treatment and sanitation is slow. Many people around the world still lack sanitation and even basic handwashing facilities. In the OECD area, the provision of wastewater treatment services and public access to such services have continuously improved since the 1980s. Connection rates to a public wastewater treatment plant and the level of treatment vary significantly across OECD countries due to varying settlement patterns, economic and environmental conditions, starting dates and the rate at which infrastructure and maintenance work is done. More than one third of OECD countries have over 80% of their population connected to a sewage treatment plant with secondary or

tertiary treatment. Primary treatment remains widespread in some countries, and a few still lag behind with 20% of their population unconnected to sewage treatment.

In many countries, the main challenge now is to ensure proper financing for renewing and upgrading existing and often ageing networks and treatment plants. Some countries have reached the economic and technical limits in terms of sewerage and connection rates; they must find other means to serve small, isolated settlements, including through effective independent on-site treatment systems. Overall, more efforts need to be made to increase advanced wastewater treatment where economically viable and environmentally justified, and to cope with new and emerging pollutants such as pharmaceutical residues or microplastics.

Figure 10. Most people living in OECD countries benefit from public wastewater treatment

Sewage treatment connection rates, 2017 or latest year

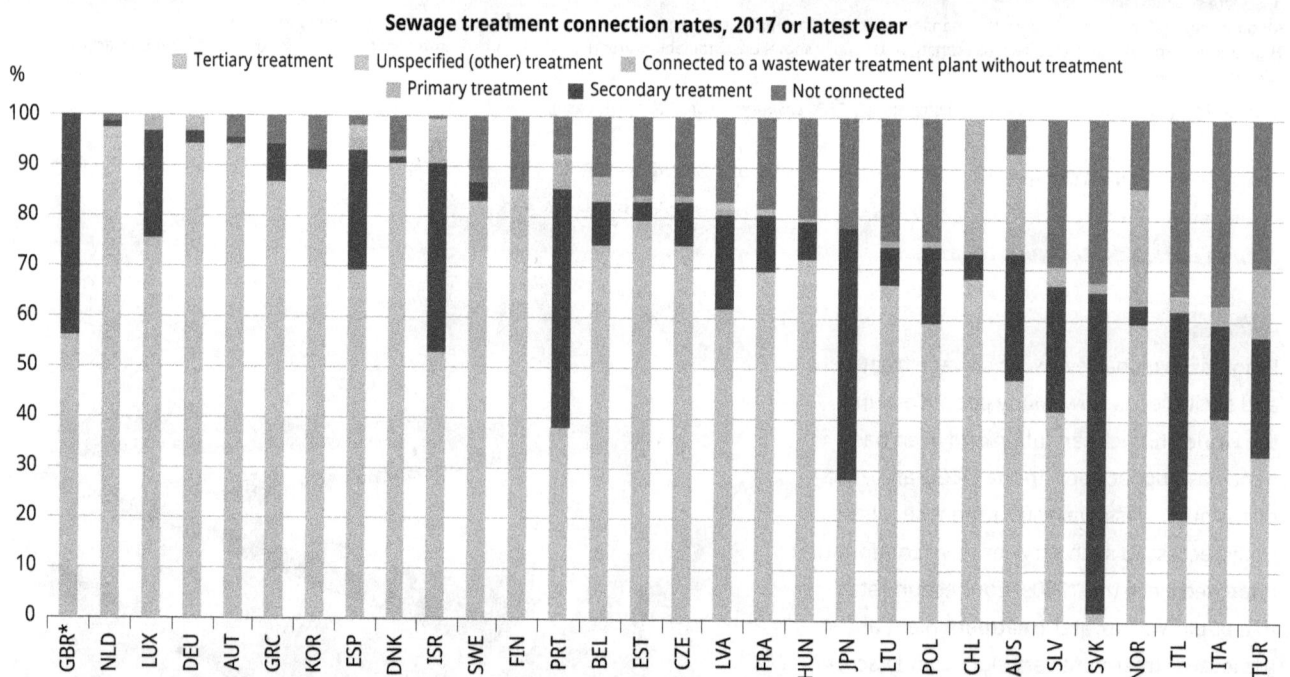

Legend: Tertiary treatment · Unspecified (other) treatment · Connected to a wastewater treatment plant without treatment · Primary treatment · Secondary treatment · Not connected

Countries (left to right): GBR*, NLD, LUX, DEU, AUT, GRC, KOR, ESP, DNK, ISR, SWE, FIN, PRT, BEL, EST, CZE, LVA, FRA, HUN, JPN, LTU, POL, CHL, AUS, SLV, SVK, NOR, ITL, ITA, TUR

Note:
Primary treatment: physical and/or chemical process involving settlement of suspended solids, or other process in which the BOD5 of the incoming wastewater is reduced by at least 20% before discharge and the total suspended solids are reduced by at least 50%.
Secondary treatment: process generally involving biological treatment with a secondary settlement or other process, with a BOD removal of at least 70% and a COD removal of at least 75%.
Tertiary treatment: treatment of nitrogen and/or phosphorous and/or any other pollutant affecting the quality or a specific use of water (microbiological pollution, colour etc.).
*England & Wales only

Source: OECD (2019), "Water: Wastewater treatment", *OECD Environment Statistics* (database).

BOX 3. MANAGING PHARMACEUTICAL RESIDUES IN FRESHWATER

About 2 000 active pharmaceutical ingredients (APIs) are being administered worldwide in prescription medicines, non-prescription drugs and veterinary drugs. Their residues are of increasing environmental concern. APIs are found in surface waters, groundwater, drinking water, soil, manure, biota, sediment and the food chain. They originate from the formulation and production of pharmaceutical products, from their consumption and excretion, and from inadequate management and disposal of unused or expired products. Most enter the environment through the discharge of untreated household wastewater and effluents from wastewater treatment plants. Industry and intensive agriculture and aquaculture can be important emission sources locally.

Pharmaceutical residues in the environment raise particular environmental concerns because they interact with living systems at low doses; they are very slow to degrade or are continuously released into the environment at rates exceeding degradation rates. Hormones, antibiotics, analgesics, antidepressants and anticancer pharmaceuticals used for human health; and hormones, antibiotics and parasiticides used as veterinary pharmaceuticals are particularly worrying.

The concentrations and impacts of pharmaceuticals in the environment depend on a combination of variables, including their use, the toxicity, degradation, persistence and mobility properties of the pharmaceutical; source and timing of pollution; wastewater treatment plant technology, operation and removal efficiency; agriculture and veterinary practices; and the sensitivity of the receiving environment and exposure history. Environmental risk assessment of pharmaceuticals is uncertain due to lack of knowledge concerning the fate of APIs in the environment, impacts on ecosystems and human health, and the effects of mixtures of pharmaceuticals and other chemicals.

Pharmaceuticals can have unintended, negative impacts on aquatic organisms and ecosystems, including mortality; changes to physiology, behaviour and reproduction. APIs from oral contraceptives can for example cause feminisation of fish and amphibians; psychiatric drugs can alter fish behaviour making them less risk-averse and vulnerable to predators; antibiotics exacerbate the problem of antimicrobial resistance – declared by the World Health Organisation as a global health crisis, projected to cause more deaths globally than cancer by 2050.

Managing pharmaceutical residues in fresh water is challenging. Current policy approaches are inadequate for protecting water quality and freshwater ecosystems. What is needed is a combination of policies and instruments that address the full life-cycle of these substances and that involve all stakeholders along the pharmaceutical chain (public authorities, industry, consumers). A recent OECD study calls for a better understanding of the effects of pharmaceutical residues in the environment, greater international collaboration and accountability distribution, and effective policy actions.

Source: OECD (2019), *Pharmaceutical Residues in Freshwater: Hazards and Policy Responses*, OECD Studies on Water, OECD Publishing, Paris, https://doi.org/10.1787/c936f42d-en.

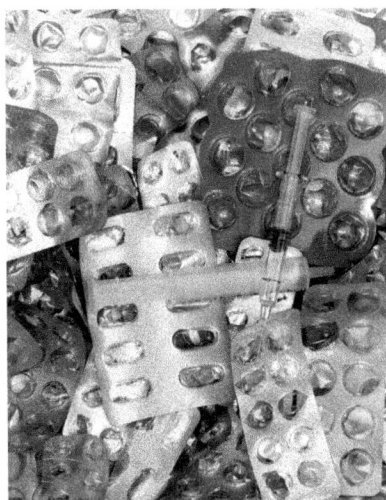

4 CIRCULAR ECONOMY, WASTE AND MATERIALS

Material resources form the physical foundation of the economy. Their extraction, processing and use have environmental, economic and social consequences in countries and beyond national borders. Circular economy and sustainable materials management are key to avoiding the waste of finite materials and risking their inefficient use in the economy.

Progress is measured through indicators on the use of materials, the generation of waste and the recovery of materials from waste.

Electronic waste recycling plant in Izmit, Turkey
Photo © OVKNHR/Shutterstock.com

THE ISSUE

Material resources form the physical foundation of the economy, and are an important source of income and jobs. They differ in their physical and chemical characteristics, their abundance and their value to countries. The extraction of raw materials from natural resources and the related production and consumption processes have environmental, economic and social consequences in countries and beyond national borders. The intensity and nature of these consequences depend on the kind and amounts of natural resources and materials used, the stage of the resource cycle at which they occur, the way the material resources are used and managed, and the type and location of the natural environment from where they originate.

Economic growth generally implies growing demand for raw materials, energy and other natural resources, and growing amounts of materials that risk ending up as waste if not properly managed. Main concerns relate to the pressures exerted on natural assets, the negative environmental impacts from the extraction, processing and use of materials and from inappropriate waste management on human health and the environment (e.g. air, soil and water pollution, climate change, degradation of natural habitats and ecosystems).

Establishing a resource efficient and circular economy is central to achieving green growth and sustainable development.

POLICY CHALLENGES

The main challenge for countries is to improve resource efficiency at all stages of the material lifecycle (extraction, transport, manufacturing, consumption, recovery and disposal) and throughout the supply chain. This requires broadening the scope of waste management policies in line with the waste hierarchy, which ranks waste prevention as the most preferred option that can be encouraged through eco-design, reuse, repair, refurbishment, re-manufacturing, and extended producer responsibility schemes. It also requires effective integration of policies on materials, product and chemicals management, and the use of life-cycle oriented waste, materials and product management. Examples are 3R policies (reduce, reuse, recycle), sustainable materials management, sustainable manufacturing, resource efficiency and circular economy policies.

Establishing a resource efficient and circular economy is central to achieving green growth and sustainable development. It is the way to ensure adequate supplies of materials; to manage the environmental impacts associated with their lifecycle and supply chain; and to make sure that natural resources are not degraded and remain available for future generations.

WHAT IS A CIRCULAR ECONOMY?

A CIRCULAR ECONOMY SEEKS TO:
- maximise the value of the materials and products that circulate within the economy;
- minimise material consumption, paying particular attention to virgin materials, hazardous substances, and waste streams that raise specific concerns (such as plastics, food, electric and electronic goods);
- prevent waste from being generated;
- reduce hazardous components in waste and products.

Recovering materials from waste streams for recycling or reuse, using products longer and increasing the use intensity of goods through sharing economy approaches like car-sharing are some of the areas in which circular business models are operating.

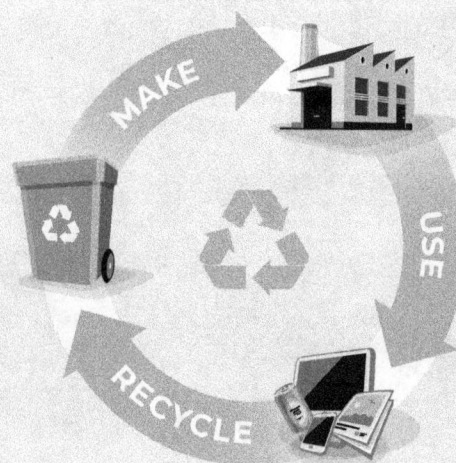

MEASURING PERFORMANCE AND PROGRESS

Environmental performance can be assessed against domestic objectives and international goals and commitments. Sustainable waste and materials management is part of the 2030 Agenda for Sustainable Development (New York, September 2015) under Goal 8 "Promote inclusive and sustainable economic growth, employment and decent work for all", Goal 12 "Ensure sustainable consumption and production patterns" and Goal 14 "Conserve and sustainably use the oceans, seas and marine resources for sustainable development". Absolute decoupling of materials use and environmental degradation from GDP growth is targeted in SDG 8.4. The sustainable management and efficient use of natural resources is targeted in SDG 12.2. The prevention and reduction of marine pollution, including marine debris is targeted in SDG 14.1. Agreements and regulations on waste in general and transfrontier movements of hazardous waste in particular, include directives of the European Union, OECD Decisions and Recommendations and the Basel Convention that was amended in 2019 to cover plastic waste. G8 and G7 countries adopted several plans and strategies related to the resource cycle, resource productivity and life-cycle based materials management. Resource efficiency was part of the G20 agenda in 2017.

MAIN TRENDS AND RECENT DEVELOPMENTS

The last decades have witnessed unprecedented growth in demands for raw materials worldwide, driven by the rapid industrialisation of emerging economies and continued high levels of material consumption in developed countries. International commodity markets have expanded, with increasing international trade flows, and increasing mobility and fragmentation of production. This has been accompanied by increases in, and volatility of, commodity prices, and by growing competition for selected raw materials.

KEY MESSAGES ON CIRCULAR ECONOMY

- Global demand for raw materials has been rising over the past decades driven by the industrialisation of emerging economies, continued high levels of material consumption in high-income countries and a growing world population. The amount of materials extracted globally doubled between 1980 and 2010, mostly driven by the rise of construction and industrial materials, and is projected to double again by 2060.

- OECD countries are moving towards higher material productivity and lower material consumption per capita. But levels of material consumption per capita remain high compared to those of other world regions. And productivity gains are more modest once all raw materials needed to satisfy final demand are considered, including those extracted abroad and embodied in international trade. The consumption of raw materials, also called the material footprint, is often higher than domestic material consumption and is growing.

- At the same time, the amounts of waste generated continue to grow in most OECD countries; only a few have managed to decouple the waste they produce from economic growth. The developments are more positive for municipal waste whose growth rate slowed down in the 2000s. A person living in the OECD area generates on average 520 kg of municipal waste per year; this is 30 kg less than in 2000, but 20 kg more than in 1990.

- The treatment of waste has improved and materials are increasingly fed back into the economy through recovery and recycling. However, much material is still lost to the economy or recycled into low value products, and landfilling remains the major disposal method in many OECD countries.

Figure 11. Projected global changes, 2011-2060

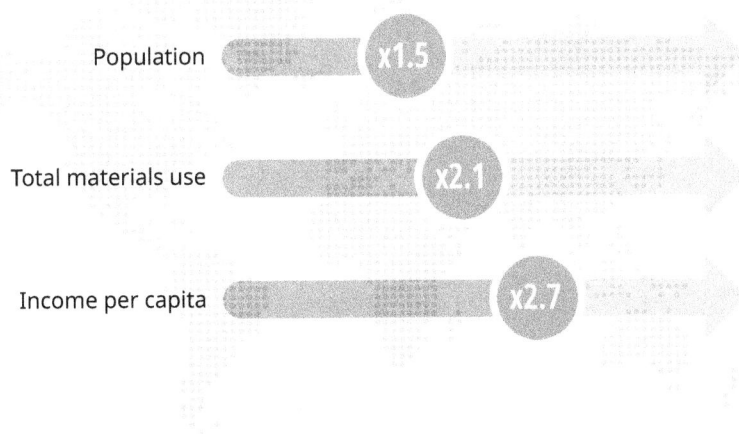

Population   x1.5

Total materials use   x2.1

Income per capita   x2.7

Source: OECD, 2019.

WHAT ARE THE ENVIRONMENTAL CONSEQUENCES OF MATERIALS USE?

The economic activities that drive materials use affect the environment in many ways. Environmental consequences stem from obtaining the materials (e.g. greenhouse gas emissions from extracting and processing primary raw materials), from their use (e.g. air pollution caused by burning fossil fuels), and from their disposal (e.g. pollution of air, soil and water from landfills).

Life-cycle analysis of global extraction and production of seven metals (iron, aluminium, copper, zinc, lead, nickel and manganese) and two construction materials (concrete, and sand and gravel) by the OECD shows a wide range of environmental consequences, including impacts on acidification, climate change, cumulative energy demand, eutrophication, human toxicity, land use, ozone layer depletion, photochemical oxidation, and toxicity of ecosystems. The seven metals and two construction materials together represent almost one quarter of all GHG emissions and one sixth of cumulative energy demand.

Overall, materials extraction, processing and use generate more than half of all greenhouse gas emissions globally.

Source: OECD 2019.

By 2060 the global economy is projected to quadruple and global material use to double.

The amount of materials extracted doubled between 1980 and 2010, mostly driven by the rise of construction and industrial materials (OECD 2015). In the coming decades, demands for raw materials are projected to increase further though at a slower pace thanks to structural change and technology developments. By 2060 the global economy is projected to quadruple and global material use to double (OECD 2019).

In the OECD area material consumption, in terms of domestic material consumption (DMC), increased along with economic growth in the 1990s, and at a slower pace as of the 2000s revealing a decoupling from GDP. About 19 Gt of materials are consumed per year; almost half of them in the OECD America region. Non-metallic minerals, mostly for construction, and fossil energy carriers represent the most important share, followed by biomass.

Figure 12. Material use has stabilised in the OECD area, but continues to grow worldwide

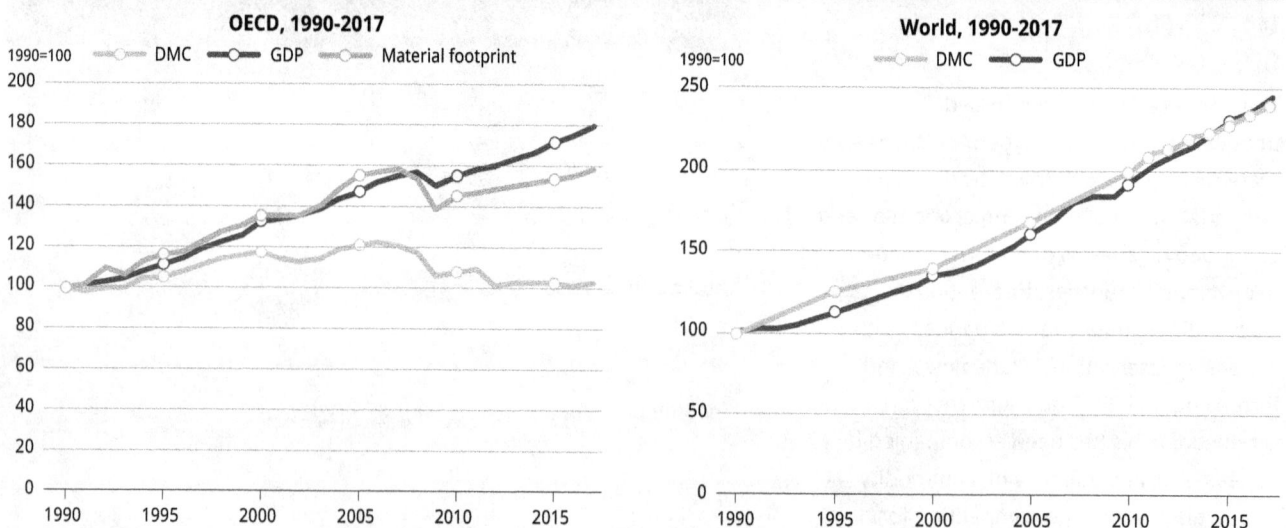

Source: OECD (2019), "Material resources", *OECD Environment Statistics* (database).

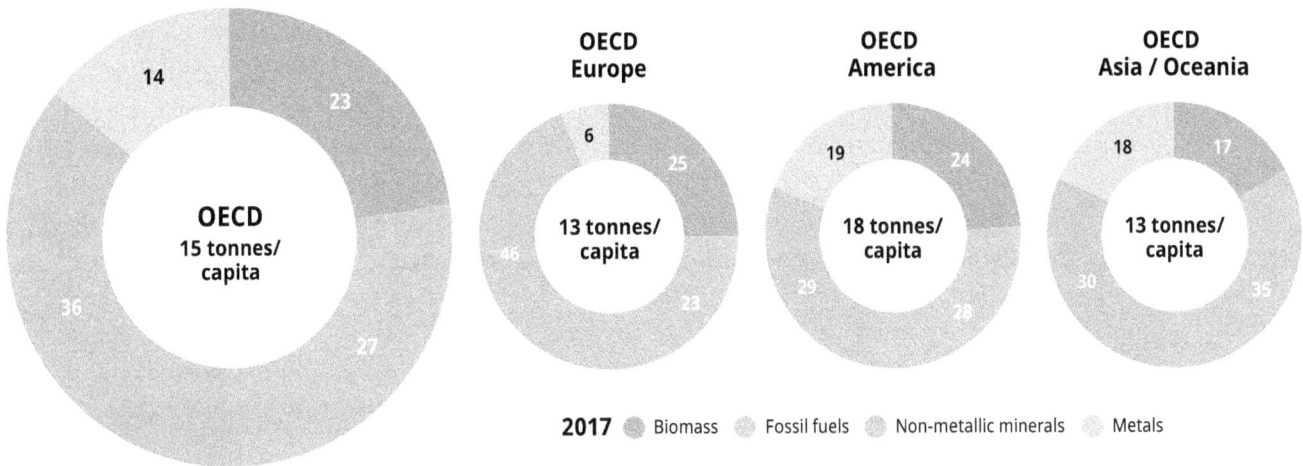

OECD
15 tonnes/
capita

14
23
36
27

OECD
Europe

13 tonnes/
capita

6
25
46
23

OECD
America

18 tonnes/
capita

19
24
29
28

OECD
Asia / Oceania

13 tonnes/
capita

18
17
30
35

2017 ● Biomass ● Fossil fuels ● Non-metallic minerals ● Metals

Source: OECD (2019), "Material resources", *OECD Environment Statistics* (database).

Since 2000, material intensity per capita has decreased in most OECD countries. In some countries, such as the Baltic countries, per capita material consumption increased driven by economic growth and infrastructure development associated with a declining population. A person living in an OECD country consumes on average about 15 tonnes of materials per year. This is 22% less than in 2000 (19 tonnes per person), but still higher than in other world regions (about 12 tonnes per person). In the coming decades consumption levels in emerging and developing economies are expected to progressively converge with current OECD levels, driven by growing populations and higher incomes and living standards.

Since 2000, the vast majority of OECD countries have experienced improvements in material productivity. Today, OECD countries generate on average USD 2 600 per tonne of materials consumed, compared to USD 1 700 per tonne in 2000. This reflects efficiency gains in production processes, changes in the materials mix and the substitution of domestic production with imports. It also reflects a decreasing demand for materials following the 2008

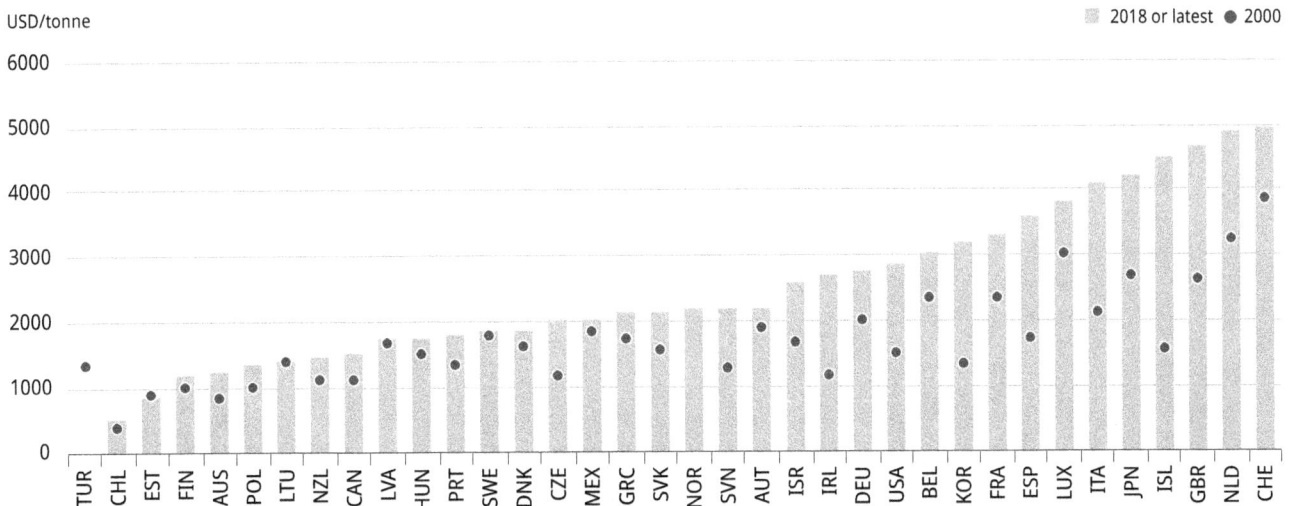

USD/tonne

■ 2018 or latest ● 2000

Chart showing values from 0 to 6000 USD/tonne for countries: TUR, CHL, EST, FIN, AUS, POL, LTU, NZL, CAN, LVA, HUN, PRT, SWE, DNK, CZE, MEX, GRC, SVK, NOR, SVN, AUT, ISR, IRL, DEU, USA, BEL, KOR, FRA, ESP, LUX, ITA, JPN, ISL, GBR, NLD, CHE

Source: OECD (2019), "Material resources", *OECD Environment Statistics* (database).

financial crisis that led to reduced economic output. As economic growth resumed, domestic material consumption remained stable in many countries.

Once all raw materials needed to satisfy final demand in OECD countries, including those extracted abroad and embodied in international trade of goods are considered, productivity gains are more modest. The raw material consumption or material footprint of the OECD area increased by 60% since 1990 and reached almost 33 Gt in 2017. The per capita footprint, is generally higher (25 tonnes per person on average) than DMC per capita (15 tonnes per person on average), but follows a similar trend. Countries with high import rates and high-income levels usually show higher footprints.

At the same time, many materials still end up as waste and risk getting lost to the economy. Waste from all sources continues to grow in most countries, generally in line with population and economic growth with a few exceptions (e.g. France, Hungary, Japan, Slovak Republic, Spain). The amounts of waste produced, their composition and their origin vary among countries; they relate to the structure of the economy and the level of investment in innovation and cleaner technologies. In many countries, information remains insufficient to monitor total waste streams, their recovery and the use of secondary raw materials in the economy. Estimates indicate that in 2016, close to 12% of the material resources used in the European Union came from recycled products and recovered materials, which saved primary raw materials from being extracted (Eurostat 2019).

The developments are more positive for municipal waste. Municipal solid waste

WHAT IS RAW MATERIAL CONSUMPTION?

Raw material consumption, also called material footprint, represents the portion of raw materials extracted anywhere in the world (global extraction) that are needed to satisfy final demand of an economy. It includes materials that are directly used by an economy in the form of raw materials, semi-processed materials or processed goods, and materials that are associated with the production of imported goods but not physically imported.

generated in the OECD area has risen mostly in line with private consumption expenditure and GDP during the 1990s; this rise has been slowing down as of the early 2000s. Today, the amounts generated exceed an estimated 675 million tonnes. A person living in the OECD area generates on average 520 kg of waste per year; this is 20 kg more than in 1990, but 30 kg less than in 2000. The amount and composition of municipal waste vary widely among OECD countries, being related to levels and patterns of consumption, the rate of urbanisation, lifestyles, and national waste management practices. Europeans generate on average about 110 kg less than people living in the Americas but 100 kg more than people living in the OECD Asia-Oceania region. Worldwide, an estimated 2 billion tonnes of municipal waste were generated in 2016 (an average of 270 kg per person) and this amount is expected to grow further (World Bank, 2019).

OECD countries put significant **efforts into curbing municipal waste generation and improving management methods**. Mechanical and biological pre-treatment is used to facilitate recovery, enhance incineration efficiency, and reduce the amounts being landfilled. Manufacturers are encouraged or required to accept responsibility for their products after the point of sale. European Union member states, Japan and other countries have introduced recovery and recycling targets and monitor progress through indicators.

These efforts have started to pay off. More and more waste is being diverted from landfills and incinerators and fed back into the economy through recycling, composting and incineration with energy recovery. Several countries recycle more than one third of the municipal waste they manage (Australia, Belgium, Germany, Ireland, Korea, Slovenia). The share of municipal waste landfilled thus decreased from 61% to 42% between 1995 and 2017. Some European countries no longer landfill municipal waste (Switzerland, Germany, Finland, Sweden, Belgium). Landfilling nonetheless remains the major disposal method in several OECD countries, and many materials recovered from the waste stream continue to be used as low value products (e.g. construction and demolition waste used for backfilling).

More and more waste is being diverted from landfills and incinerators and fed back into the economy through recycling, composting and incineration with energy recovery.

Figure 15. The treatment of municipal solid waste has improved

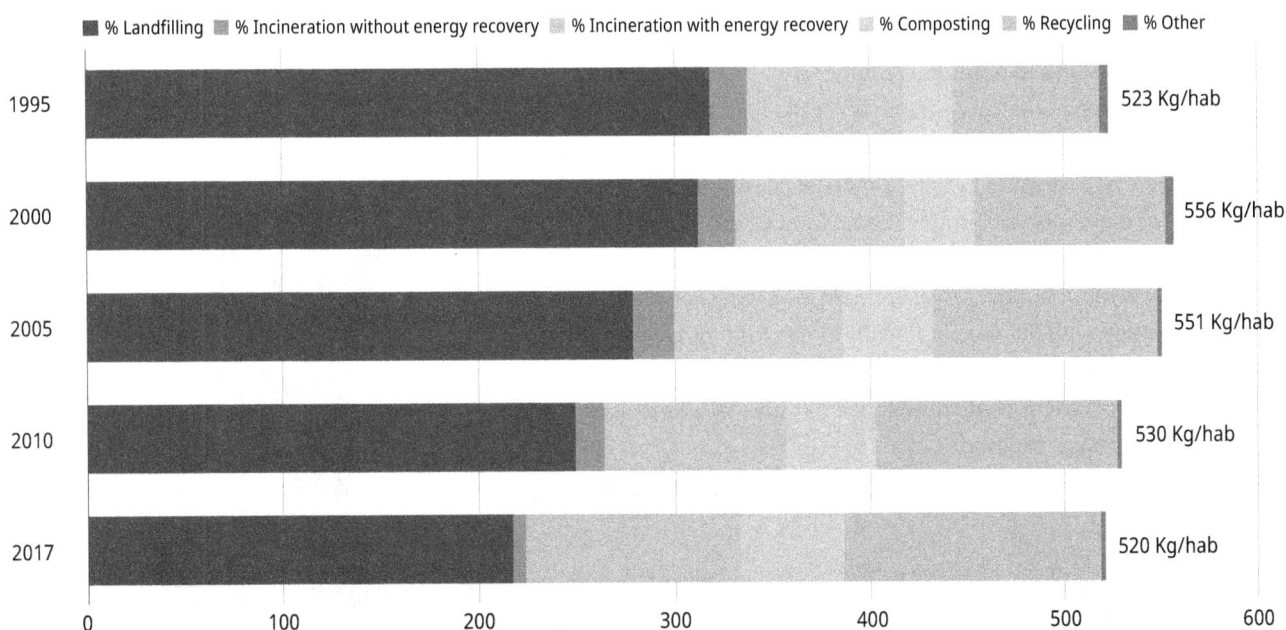

■ % Landfilling ■ % Incineration without energy recovery ▦ % Incineration with energy recovery ▦ % Composting ▦ % Recycling ■ % Other

1995	523 Kg/hab
2000	556 Kg/hab
2005	551 Kg/hab
2010	530 Kg/hab
2017	520 Kg/hab

Source: OECD (2019), "Waste: Municipal waste", *OECD Environment Statistics* (database).

Recycling and recovery rates

%   Recycling   Other recovery   2000, recovery rates

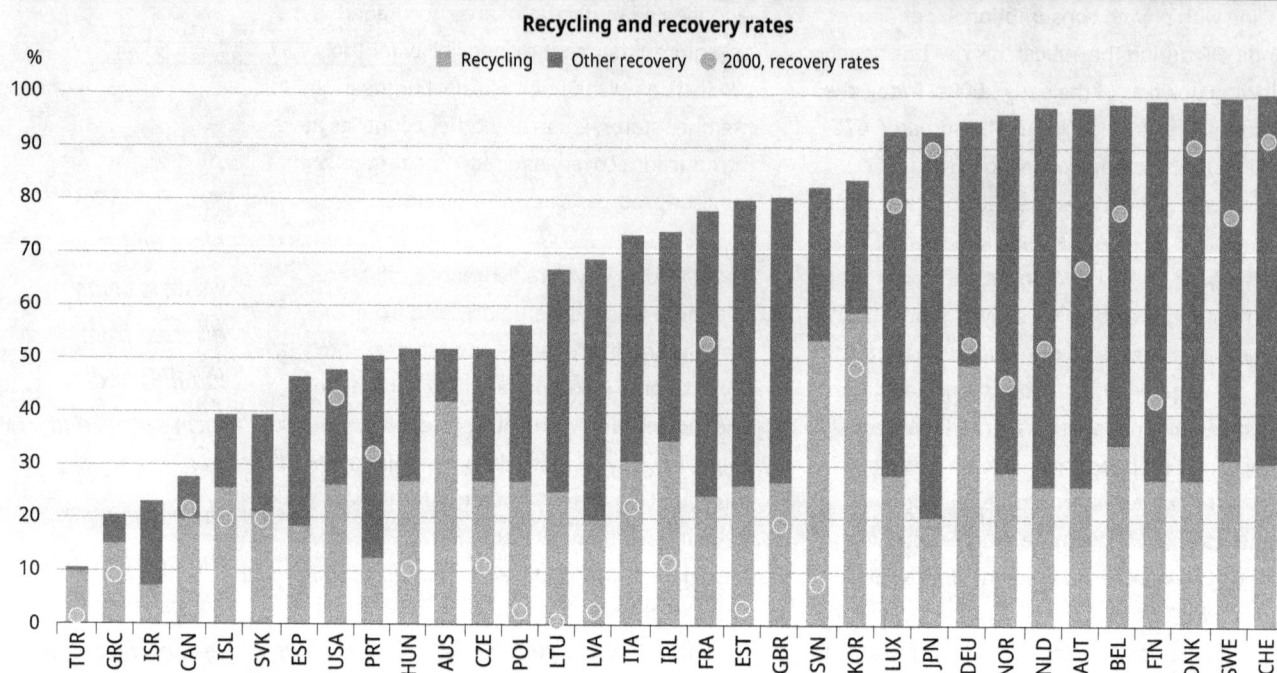

Note: Other recovery includes composting and incineration with energy recovery.

Source: OECD (2019), "Waste: Municipal waste", *OECD Environment Statistics* (database).

Countries also pay increasingly attention to waste streams that contain hazardous components or high-value materials, that raise particular concerns as to their negative environmental impacts and that require special management. Examples include food waste, waste electrical and electronic equipment, construction and demolition waste, end-of-life vehicles, batteries and plastic waste. Policy action to prevent waste from being generated and to establish circular business models is more recent in most OECD countries, but is gaining momentum.

WASTE ELECTRICAL AND ELECTRONIC EQUIPMENT (WEEE) or e-waste contains high-value and hazardous components such as lead, rare earths, gold, copper, mercury, lithium and palladium that require special management. About 45 million tonnes of e-waste are generated in the world. This is equivalent to 125 000 jumbo jets or 4 500 Eiffel Towers. About 19 of these 45 million tonnes come from OECD countries (43%). The amounts of e-waste and intensities per capita are growing rapidly, raising questions about their management. The collection and recovery of e-waste is improving but remains insufficient in front of growing demands for electrical and electronic equipment. In many countries, e-waste is still landfilled or collected and dismantled by informal waste pickers, and illegal trade remains an issue.

Source: Baldé, C.P. et al. (2017), The Global E-waste Monitor, United Nations University (UNU), International Telecommunication Union (ITU) & International Solid Waste Association (ISWA), Bonn/Geneva/Vienna.

Platform for accelerating the circular economy and World economic forum, (2019), A New Circular Vision for Electronics Time for a Global Reboot,http://www3.weforum.org/docs/WEF_A_New_Circular_Vision_for_Electronics.pdf.

BOX 4. A CLOSER LOOK AT PLASTIC WASTE

Plastics are ubiquitous in everyday life and their use has grown quickly since the 1950s. Some common examples include: films used in packaging, fibres used in textiles, durable plastics used in vehicles, consumer goods or construction. Plastics are produced from chemicals derived from fossil fuels. Half of them are designed for single use and are then expected to be discarded. The production, use and disposal of plastics have many environmental consequences, from carbon and pollutant emissions to leakage into soil, freshwater and oceans. These consequences depend on the type of plastic and on whether plastic waste is properly managed.

Plastic waste raises concerns because of its physical and chemical properties. Plastics are durable, resistant to degradation and can remain in the environment for centuries. They often contain chemical additives that entail environmental and health risks, and are generally comingled with food residues, paper and other materials. At least eight types of plastic polymers are widely used and found in waste, mainly low-density polyethylene (used for packaging) and polypropylene (used for hinges, textiles, medical equipment). These materials are recyclable, but often mismanaged.

About 300 million tonnes of plastic waste is generated every year globally. Every year, more than 8 million tonnes of plastic end up in the ocean. They come from marine-based sources (fishing, shipment, cruises) and land-based sources (e.g. tourism, households, agriculture, retail) often due to failures in waste management and in wastewater treatment. 80% of all marine litter is plastics. If current trends continue, there could be more plastics in the ocean than fish by 2050.

Plastics threaten marine ecosystems. They can absorb persistent bio-accumulative and toxic substances, and act as a potential vector for disease. Plastics can travel thousands of kilometres with ocean currents and be found anywhere in the world, including remote islands, the poles and the deep seas. Large debris can transport invasive alien species across oceans. Single-use or disposable plastics are of special concern as they often contain micro-plastics or break up into micro-plastics. Small debris are particularly harmful as animals

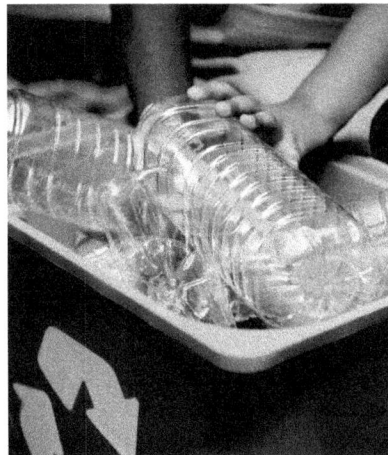

mistake them for food and allow some of their components move up the food chain with risks for human health. Research shows that more than 800 marine and coastal species are affected through ingestion, entanglement, ghost fishing or dispersal by rafting.

Measures to address the environmental impacts of plastics include waste prevention, material substitution, more effective waste management, improved plastics design, and more advanced wastewater treatment that eliminates micro-plastics. To cover all stages of the plastics value chain, a mix of policy instruments is needed (market-based and regulatory instruments, information tools, etc.). The OECD has investigated how better functioning markets for recycled plastics could stimulate higher collection and recycling rates and how effective policies to prevent single-use plastic waste are from an environmental, economic and behavioural point of view.

Sources:
Ellen MacArthur Foundation (2017), *The New Plastics Economy, Rethinking the Future of Plastics and Catalysing Action*, https://www.ellenmacarthurfoundation.org/assets/downloads/publications/NPEC-Hybrid_English_22-11- 17_Digital.pdf.

OECD (2020 forthcoming), *Preventing single-use plastic waste: implications of different policy approaches*, OECD Publishing, Paris.

OECD (2018), *Improving Plastics Management: Trends, policy responses, and the role of international co-operation and trade*, Background report prepared for the G7 Environment, Energy and Oceans Ministers. https://www.oecd.org/environment/waste/policy-highlights-improving-plastics-management.pdf.

SCBD (2016), *CBD Technical Series No 83*, Marine debris: Understanding, preventing and mitigating the significant adverse impacts on marine and coastal biodiversity, Secretariat of the Convention on Biological Diversity, https://www.cbd.int/doc/publications/cbd-ts-83-en.pdf.

5 BIOLOGICAL RESOURCES AND BIODIVERSITY

Biological resources and their diversity provide key resources and services for the economy and play an essential role in maintaining life-support systems and quality of life. Preserving biodiversity is fundamental to sustainable development.

Progress is measured through indicators on threatened species, protected areas, forest resources and changes in land cover.

Boreal forest in Russia
Photo © Vladimir Melnikov/Shutterstock.com

THE ISSUE

Biological resources are essential elements of ecosystems and of natural capital. They provide raw materials for many sectors of the economy. Their diversity plays an essential role in providing ecosystem services and in maintaining life-support systems and quality of life. Preserving this diversity is hence key to sustainable development.

The loss of biodiversity is a key concern nationally and globally. It reduces ecosystem resilience and increases vulnerability to threats such as the negative impacts of climate change. Pressures on biodiversity can be physical (e.g. habitat alteration and fragmentation through changes in land use and sea use, and changes in land cover, over-exploitation of natural resources), chemical (toxic contamination, acidification, oil spills, other pollution from human activities) or biological (e.g. alteration of population dynamics and species structure through invasive alien species or the commercial use of wildlife resources). Other factors that play a role are changes in climate and weather conditions.

The loss of biodiversity is a key concern nationally and globally. It reduces ecosystem resilience and increases vulnerability to threats such as the negative impacts of climate change.

WHAT IS BIODIVERSITY?

"Biological diversity" means the variability among living organisms from all sources including, inter alia, terrestrial, marine and other aquatic ecosystems and the ecological complexes of which they are part; this includes diversity within species, between species and of ecosystems.

"Biological resources" includes genetic resources, organisms or parts thereof, populations, or any other biotic component of ecosystems with actual or potential use or value for humanity.

Source: Convention on Biological Diversity.

POLICY CHALLENGES

The main challenge is to ensure effective conservation and sustainable use of biodiversity. This implies strengthening the degree of protection of species, habitats and terrestrial and aquatic ecosystems, including oceans. Strategies include eliminating illegal exploitation and trade of endangered species, eliminating illegal, unreported and unregulated fishing, putting in place ambitious policy mixes (regulatory approaches, economic instruments, information, voluntary approaches); and integrating biodiversity concerns into economic and sectoral policies. Biodiversity preservation and restoration also requires reforming and removing environmentally harmful subsidies and strengthening the role of biodiversity-relevant taxes, fees and charges, as well as other economic instruments such as payments for ecosystem services, biodiversity offsets and tradable permits (e.g. transferable quotas for fisheries).

MEASURING PERFORMANCE AND PROGRESS

Environmental performance can be assessed against domestic objectives and international goals and commitments.

Biodiversity is part of the 2030 Agenda for Sustainable Development adopted in September 2015 under Goal 15 "Protect, restore and promote *sustainable use of terrestrial ecosystems, sustainably manage forests, combat desertification, and halt and reverse land degradation and halt biodiversity loss" and Goal 14 "Conserve and sustainably use the oceans, seas and marine resources for sustainable development".*

The main international agreement on biodiversity is the 1992 Convention on Biological Diversity. Other relevant international agreements are: the 1979 Convention on the Conservation of Migratory Species of Wild Animals, the 1973 Convention on International Trade in Endangered Species of Wild Fauna and Flora, the 1971 Convention on Wetlands of International Importance, the 1979 Convention on the Conservation of European Wildlife and Natural Habitats, and the Agreement on Port State Measures to Prevent, Deter and Eliminate Illegal, Unreported and Unregulated Fishing that entered into force in June 2016.

MAIN TRENDS AND RECENT DEVELOPMENTS

Many animal and plant species are threatened
Pressures on biodiversity continue to grow. Many natural ecosystems have been degraded, limiting the services they provide, and many animal and plant species are threatened by habitat alteration or loss, both within and outside protected areas (e.g. on farms, in forests). In most OECD countries, the number of animal and plant species identified as endangered is increasing, particularly in countries with a high population density and a high concentration of human activities. Amphibians and freshwater fish are on average more threatened than birds, plants and mammals. But specialist birds have declined by nearly 30% in 40 years, reflecting habitat degradation. The largest declines occurred in grasslands and arid lands in North America, and in farmed lands in Europe. At global level, the Red List Index shows a deterioration between 1993 and 2019, indicating that more species are at risk of extinction.

In most OECD countries, the number of animal and plant species identified as endangered is increasing.

Marine plastic litter and micro-plastics are a major threat to ocean biodiversity. More than 800 marine and coastal species are estimated to be affected through ingestion, entanglement, ghost fishing or dispersal by rafting. Between 2012 and 2016, aquatic mammal and seabird species known to be affected by marine litter ingestion increased from 26% and 38% to 40% and 44%, respectively (SCBD 2016).

The proportion of world marine fish stocks within biologically sustainable limits (target 14.4) declined from 90% in 1974 to 67% in 2015. 33% of the stocks are estimated to be fished at a biologically unsustainable level and therefore overexploited; they yield less than their maximum potential owing to pressure from excess fishing in the past. Under-fished stocks decreased continuously from 1974 and represented only 7% percent of the total assessed stocks in 2015. It should be noted that there is still a large number of stocks for which it is not yet possible to determine stock status (FAO 2018).

WHAT IS THE ROLE OF FISH RESOURCES?

Fish resources play key roles for human food supply and aquatic ecosystems. Fish represents about 20% of the animal protein consumed worldwide. Fish is among the most traded food commodities, and in many countries fisheries make an important contribution to incomes and employment opportunities.

Main pressures on fish resources include fishing, coastal development and pollution loads from land-based sources, maritime transport, and maritime dumping.

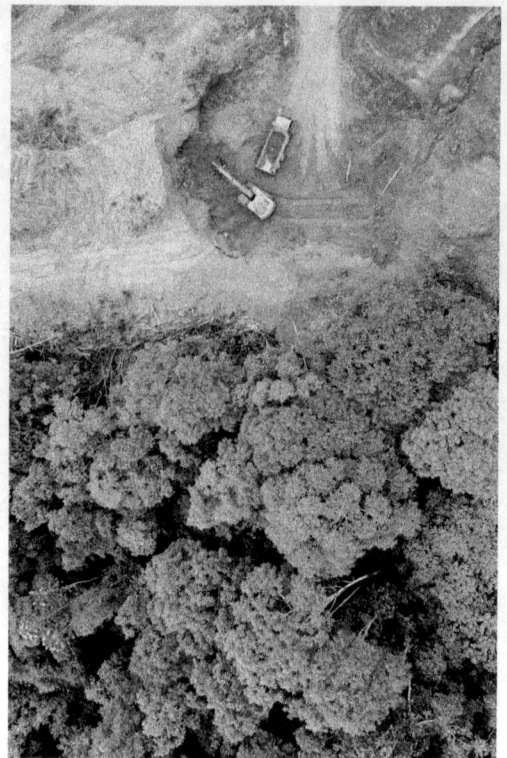

Many forests are threatened by fragmentation and degradation

Worldwide, many forest resources are threatened by overexploitation, fragmentation, degradation of environmental quality and conversion to other types of land use. Over the past decades, the area of forests and wooded land has remained stable or has slightly increased in most OECD countries. But it decreased at world level due in part to continued deforestation in tropical countries, often to provide land for agriculture, grazing and logging. Recent data suggest that global forest loss is slowing down (UNSD 2019).

About one third of the OECD area is covered by trees. Most countries show a sustainable use of their forest resources at national level, maintaining the use intensity in forest available for wood supply below 100%. Variations among and within countries are significant. In 13 out of 23 countries for which trends over a longer period are available, the intensity of use of forest resources has increased. This is partly due to the use of wood as biomass for energy that is encouraged to achieve renewable energy and climate objectives.

Intensity of use of forest resources

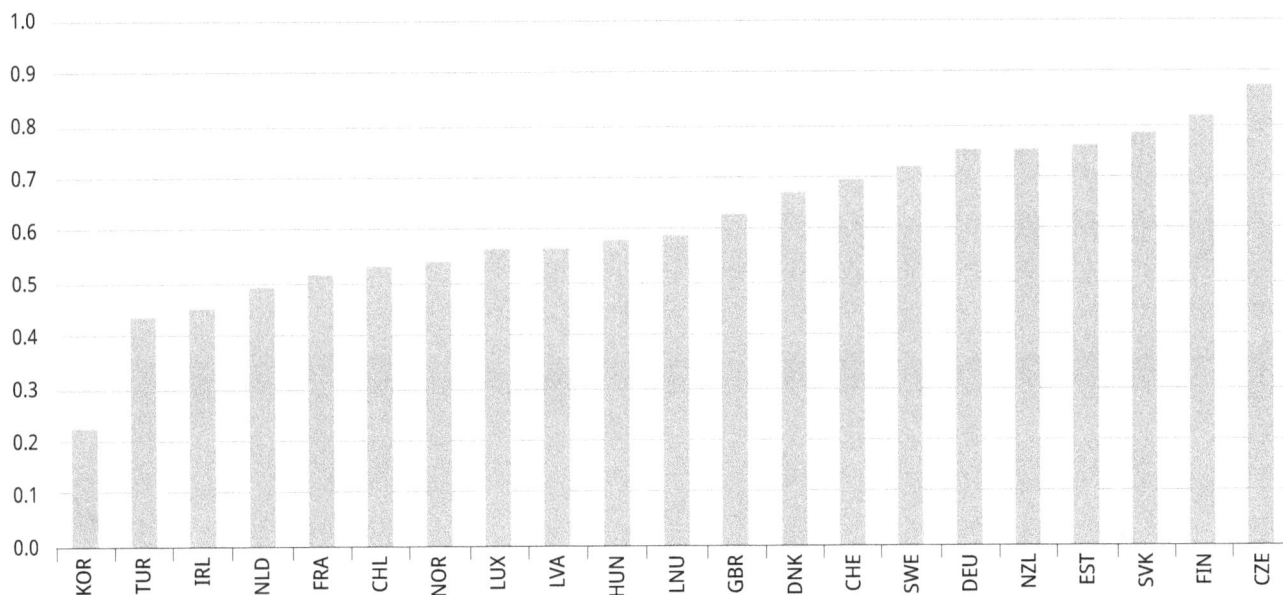

Note: Actual harvest or fellings over annual productive capacity. Korea shows a rather low intensity because its forests are young and grow rapidly (thanks to massive reforestation programmes since 1973).

Source: OECD (2019), "Forest resources", *OECD Environment Statistics* (database).

WHAT IS THE ROLE OF FOREST RESOURCES?

Forests are among the most diverse and widespread ecosystems on earth, and have many functions: they provide timber and other forest products; have cultural values; deliver recreation benefits and ecosystem services, including regulation of soil, air and water; are reservoirs for biodiversity; and act as carbon sinks. Forests are unevenly distributed. A handful of the most forest-rich countries account for the bulk of the world's forest resources. OECD countries account for about 27% of the world's forest area.

The impact of human activities on forest health and on natural forest growth and regeneration raises widespread concern. The main pressures stem from human activities, including agriculture expansion, transport infrastructure development, unsustainable forestry, air pollution, climate change and intentional burning of forests.

Protected areas are expanding

There are some encouraging developments in protecting ecosystems. Protected areas are expanding in all OECD countries and worldwide. They cover on average 16% of the land area and 25% of marine areas (i.e. exclusive economic zones - EEZ) of OECD countries, compared to respectively 11% and 5% in 2000. The areas are not however always representative of national biodiversity, nor sufficiently connected. Biodiversity outcomes and actual protection levels remain difficult to evaluate, as protected areas change over time: new areas are designated,

Figure 18. The protection of terrestrial areas has been expanding since the 1970s, the protection of marine areas expanded more recently

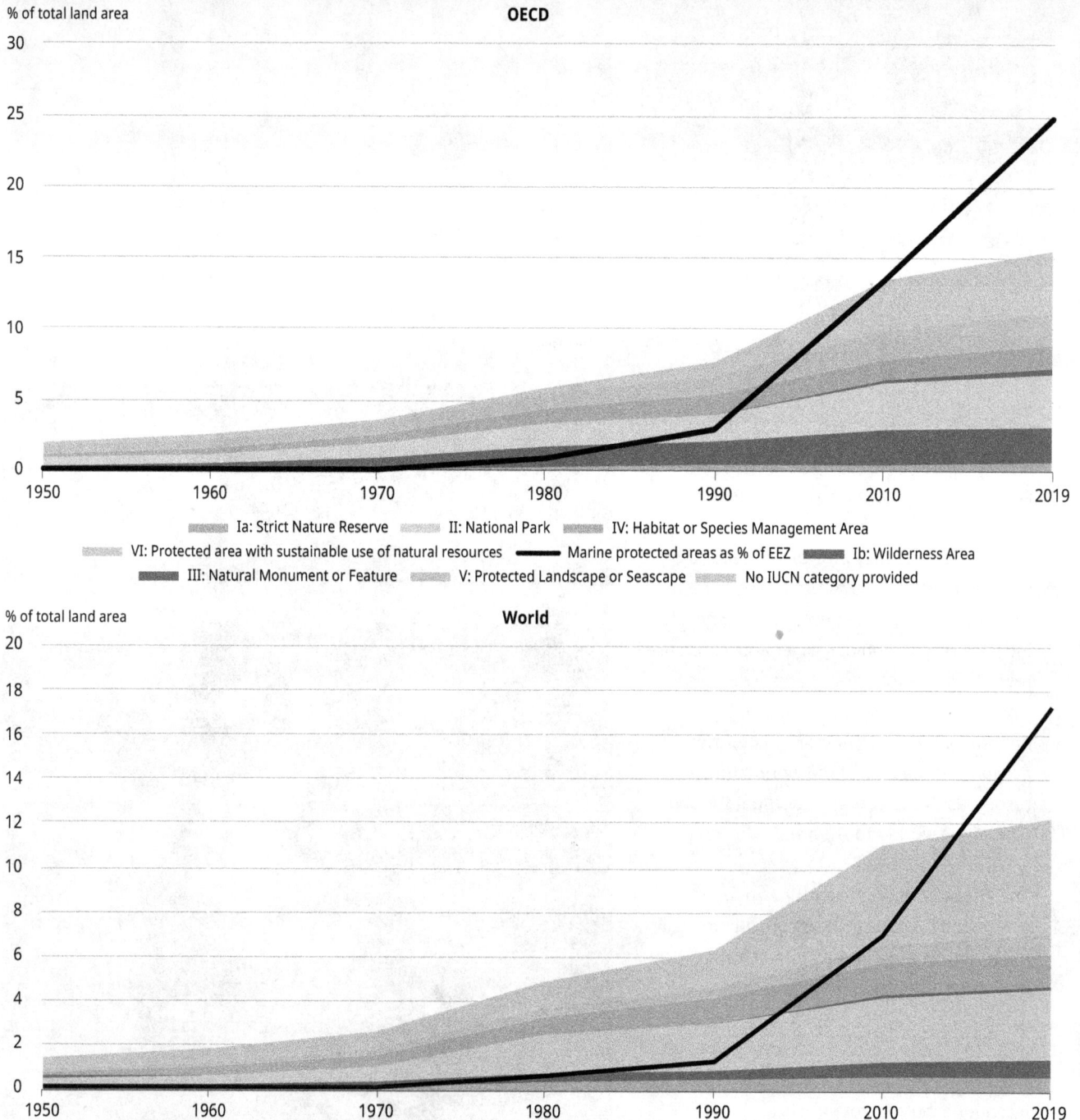

% of total land area   **OECD**

Legend:
- Ia: Strict Nature Reserve
- II: National Park
- IV: Habitat or Species Management Area
- VI: Protected area with sustainable use of natural resources
- Marine protected areas as % of EEZ
- Ib: Wilderness Area
- III: Natural Monument or Feature
- V: Protected Landscape or Seascape
- No IUCN category provided

% of total land area   **World**

Source: OECD (2019), "Biodiversity: Protected areas", *OECD Environment Statistics* (database)

boundaries are revised and some sites may be destroyed or changed by pressures from economic development or natural processes. Environmental performance depends both on the designation of the area and on management effectiveness.

According to available data, 26 OECD countries would meet the Aichi 2020 target to protect at least 17% of their land area and 18 countries would meet the target to protect at least 10% of coastal and marine areas. There are large variations among countries in the extent and the management objectives of terrestrial protected areas. These can be partly explained by differences in geography, ecology, and the pre-existing patterns of human settlement and activity on the territory. Some countries (e.g. Chile, Iceland, Luxembourg, New Zealand, Norway) have designated proportionally large areas as strict nature reserves, national parks and wilderness areas (IUCN management categories I-II). Some countries (e.g. Belgium, Israel, Luxembourg and New Zealand) use these designations to establish habitats and species management areas (categories III and IV) and others (e.g. France, Germany,

Greece, Poland, the Slovak Republic and Slovenia) to preserve cultural heritage or promote sustainable resource use (categories V and VI). Other countries use mainly regional and international designations such as the European Natura 2000 regional network (e.g. Ireland).

Worldwide, new terrestrial protected areas were designated at a consistently high rate since 1970 and now cover 13% of the land area. Designation of marine protected areas was slow until 2000. Since then, they increased by more than 22 million km² and now cover about 17% of marine areas.

Changes in land cover and infrastructure development are important drivers behind biodiversity loss
Important drivers behind biodiversity loss are changes in land use and land cover due to urbanisation and infrastructure development.

Land cover is heterogeneous across countries. In some countries cropland is dominant (Hungary, Denmark, Belgium, Turkey, Italy and France); in other countries it represents

Biodiversity outcomes and actual protection levels remain difficult to evaluate, as protected areas change over time: new areas are designated, boundaries are revised and some sites may be destroyed or changed by pressures from economic development or natural processes.

Figure 19. Grassland and cropland dominate the land cover in many countries; forests dominate in several countries

Land cover by type

Legend: Grassland, cropland | Tree cover | Sparse vegetation, shrubland, bare area | Inland water, wetland | Artificial surfaces

% of total land area

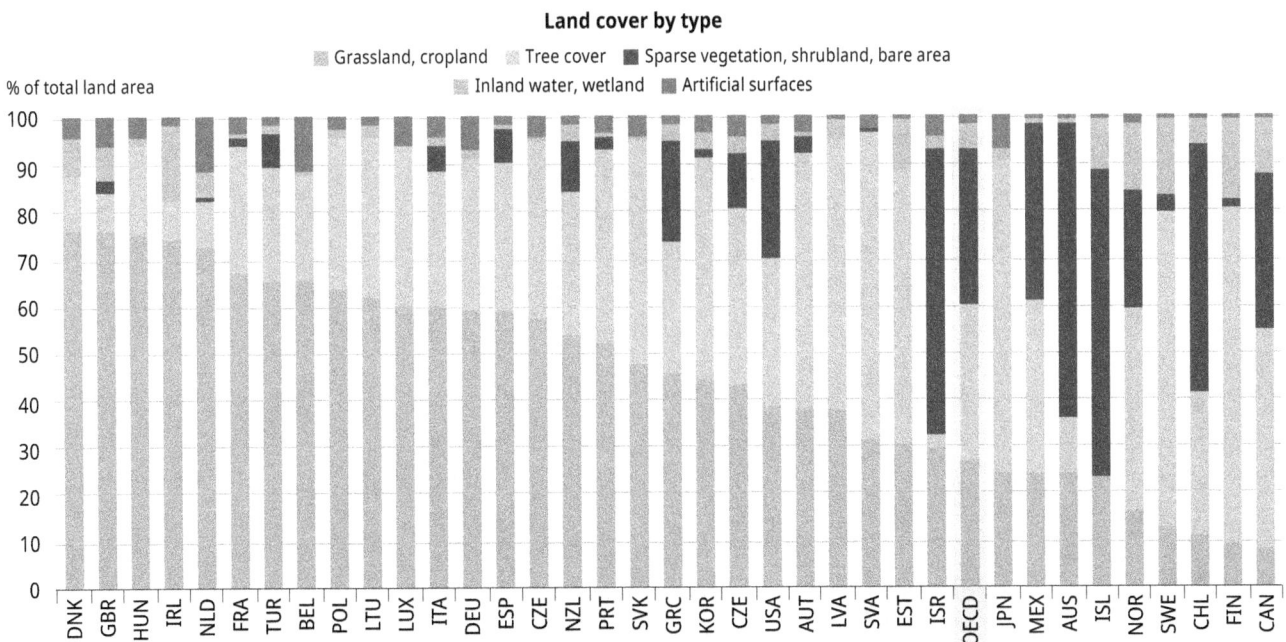

Source: OECD (2019), "Land resources: Land cover in countries and regions", *OECD Environment Statistics* (database).

less than 6% (Iceland, Norway, New-Zealand, Canada). In several countries, forests dominate the land cover (Austria, Canada, Finland, Japan, Korea, Latvia, Norway, Slovenia, Sweden).

Land covered by natural or semi-natural vegetation (i.e. land covered by trees, grasslands, wetlands, shrubland and land covered by sparse vegetation) represents more than 90% of the OECD area. These land cover types are essential for biodiversity and the provision of ecosystem services. Their area has remained broadly stable since the early 1990s with a rather small average loss of 1.4% and with variation across OECD countries ranging from 0% to 16%. This is in contrast with some other regions of the world where natural and semi-natural areas have come under intense pressure from agriculture, urbanisation, resource extraction and infrastructure. And though the average loss of natural or semi-natural vegetation is small in the OECD area, fragmentation of habitats is of concern in many countries.

Worldwide, 2.7% of (semi-) natural vegetated land has been lost to other land cover types since 1992. This represents an area of about 2.3 million km². OECD and G20 countries account for over half of this loss, which occurs primarily in Brazil, the People's Republic of China, the Russian Federation, the United States and Indonesia. Among OECD countries, the most intense losses have occurred in Korea and Israel. Most (semi-)natural land gets lost by being converted to cropland. New cropland is primarily obtained from forest areas. In some countries conversions from grassland and shrubland are important, but this may include re-cultivation of previously abandoned agricultural land.

Buildings cover about 1.1% of the total land area of OECD countries with variation across OECD countries ranging from 0.04% (Iceland) to almost 17% (Netherlands). This is 290 km² per inhabitant, 3 times the world average. Built-up areas have increased by 32% since 1990 and by 15% since 2000. Most newly built surfaces are on agricultural land, often cropland, with the exception of a few countries where development mostly takes place on areas covered by trees, grass or shrub. These developments are driven by OECD Europe, the region that has the highest built-up rate (3% of its area), whereas OECD America and OECD Asia-Oceania have rates below 1%. Globally, an area the size of the United Kingdom (244 000 km²) has been converted to built-up areas since 1990. This is an increase of 46%, mostly driven by developing countries in Africa and South East Asia.

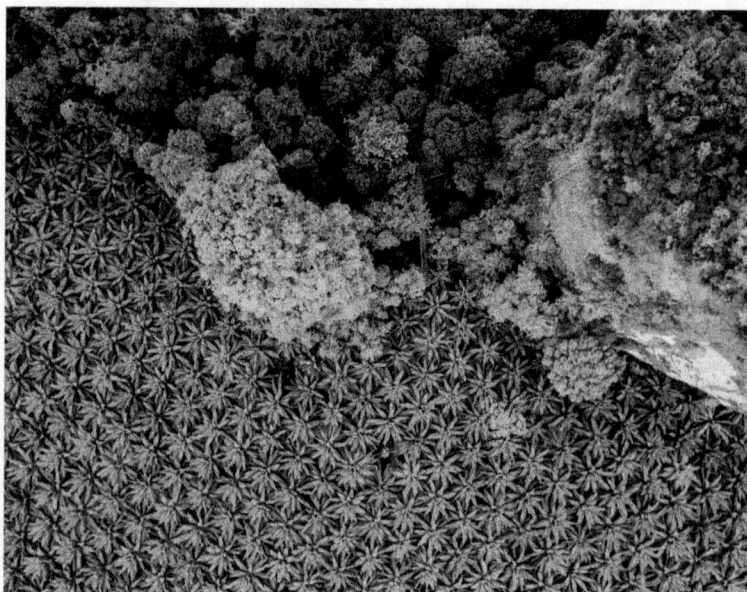

New housing development in the Czech Republic
Photo © smspsy/shutterstock.com

DATA SOURCES AND REFERENCES

Climate change

Data source

OECD, "Environment at a Glance: Climate change", *Environment at a Glance: Indicators*, https://doi.org/10.1787/5584ad47-en.

References and further reading

NOAA (2019), "Is sea level rising?", National Ocean Service website, https://oceanservice.noaa.gov/facts/sealevel.html.

OECD (2019), *Accelerating Climate Action: Refocusing Policies through a Well-being Lens*, OECD Publishing, Paris, https://doi.org/10.1787/2f4c8c9a-en.

OECD (2019), *Climate Finance Provided and Mobilised by Developed Countries in 2013-17*, OECD Publishing, Paris, https://doi.org/10.1787/39faf4a7-en.

OECD/IEA (2019), "Update on recent progress in reform of inefficient fossil-fuel subsidies that encourage wasteful consumption", https://oecd.org/fossil-fuels/publication/OECD-IEA-G20-Fossil-Fuel-Subsidies-Reform-Update-2019.pdf.

OECD (2019), *Taxing Energy Use 2019: Using Taxes for Climate Action*, OECD Publishing, Paris, https://doi.org/10.1787/058ca239-en.

OECD (2018), *Effective Carbon Rates 2018: Pricing Carbon Emissions Through Taxes and Emissions Trading*, OECD Publishing, Paris, https://doi.org/-9789264305304/10.1787en.

OECD (2018), *OECD Companion to the Inventory of Support Measures for Fossil Fuels 2018*, OECD Publishing, Paris, http://dx.doi.org/10.1787/9789264286061-en.

OECD (2015), *Aligning Policies for a Low-Carbon Economy*, OECD Publishing, Paris, http://dx.doi.org/10.1787/9789264233294-en.

UNSD (2019), *The Sustainable Development Goals Report 2019*, https://unstats.un.org/sdgs/report/2019/The-Sustainable-Development-Goals-Report-2019.pdf.

US National Oceanic and Atmospheric Administration, NOAA's Annual Greenhouse Gas Index, www.esrl.noaa.gov/gmd/aggi/.

Air quality

Data source

OECD, "Environment at a Glance: Air quality", *Environment at a Glance: Indicators*, https://doi.org/10.1787/ac4b8b89-en.

References and further reading

EEA (2019), "Air quality in Europe – 2019 report, https://www.eea.europa.eu/publications/air-quality-in-europe-2019.

Institute for Health Metrics and Evaluation (2017), "Global Burden of Disease Study 2017 Results", Seattle, United States, http://ghdx.healthdata.org/gbd-results-tool.

Mackie, A., I. Haščic and M. Cárdenas Rodríguez (2016), "Population Exposure to Fine Particles: Methodology and Results for OECD and G20 Countries", *OECD Green Growth Papers*, No. 2016/02, OECD Publishing, Paris, http://dx.doi.org/10.1787/5jlsqs8g1t9r-en.

OECD (2017), *Green Growth Indicators 2017*, OECD Green Growth Studies, OECD Publishing, Paris, https://doi.org/10.1787/9789264268586-en.

Roy, R. and N. Braathen (2017), "The Rising Cost of Ambient Air Pollution thus far in the 21st Century: Results from the BRIICS and the OECD Countries", *OECD Environment Working Papers*, No. 124, OECD Publishing, Paris, https://doi.org/10.1787/d1b2b844-en.

WHO (2019), "Air pollution: Guidelines", www.who.int/airpollution/guidelines/en/.

Freshwater resources

Data source

OECD, "Environment at a Glance: Freshwater resources", *Environment at a Glance: Indicators*, https://doi.org/10.1787/ac4b8b89-en.

References and further reading

OECD, Recommendation of the Council on Water, OECD/LEGAL/0434.

OECD (2019), *Pharmaceutical Residues in Freshwater: Hazards and Policy Responses*,

OECD Studies on Water, OECD Publishing, Paris, https://doi.org/10.1787/c936f42d-en.

OECD (2019), *Making Blended Finance Work for Water and Sanitation: Unlocking Commercial Finance for SDG 6*, OECD Studies on Water, OECD Publishing, Paris, https://doi.org/10.1787/5efc8950-en.

UNEP (2016), *A Snapshot of the World's Water Quality: Towards a global assessment*, United Nations Environment Programme, Nairobi, Kenya, https://uneplive.unep.org/media/docs/assessments/unep_wwqa_report_web.pdf.

UNEP (2019), "Chapter 9: Freshwater" in *Global Environment Outlook 6*, United Nations Environment Programme, Nairobi, Kenya, https://wedocs.unep.org/bitstream/handle/20.500.11822/27656/GEO6_CH9.pdf?sequence=1&isAllowed=y.

UNESCO WWAP (2019), *The United Nations World Water Development Report 2019: Leaving no one behind*, UNESCO, Paris, https://unesdoc.unesco.org/ark:/48223/pf0000367306.

Circular economy – waste and materials

Data source

OECD, "Environment at a Glance: Circular economy, waste and materials", *Environment at a Glance: Indicators*, https://doi.org/10.1787/ac4b8b89-en.

References and further reading

Eurostat (2019), *"What goes around comes around – EU circularity rate"*, https://ec.europa.eu/eurostat/web/products-eurostat-news/-/DDN-20190918-2.

Kaza S. et al. (2018), *What a Waste 2.0: A Global Snapshot of Solid Waste Management to 2050*, Urban Development Series, World Bank, Washington D.C., https://doi.org/10.1596/978-1-4648-1329-0.

OECD, Recommendation of the Council on Resource Productivity, OECD/LEGAL/0358.

OECD (2019), *Global Material Resources Outlook to 2060: Economic Drivers and Environmental Consequences*, OECD Publishing, Paris, https://doi.org/10.1787/9789264307452-en.

OECD (2019), *Business Models for the Circular Economy: Opportunities and Challenges for Policy*, OECD Publishing, Paris, https://doi.org/10.1787/g2g9dd62-en.

OECD (2015), *Material Resources, Productivity and the Environment*, OECD Green Growth Studies, OECD Publishing, Paris, https://doi.org/10.1787/9789264190504-en.

Biodiversity

Data source

OECD, "Environment at a Glance: Biological resources and biodiversity ", *Environment at a Glance: Indicators*, https://doi.org/10.1787/ac4b8b89-en.

References and further reading

BirdLife International, https://www.birdlife.org/.

Biodiversity Indicators Partnership (BIP) https://www.bipindicators.net/.

Convention on Biological Diversity, https://www.cbd.int/.

FAO (2018), *The State of World Fisheries and Aquaculture 2018 - Meeting the sustainable development goals,* Rome, http://www.fao.org/3/I9540EN/i9540en.pdf.

Haščič, I. and A. Mackie (2018), "Land Cover Change and Conversions: Methodology and Results for OECD and G20 Countries", *OECD Green Growth Paper*s, No. 2018/04, OECD Publishing, Paris.

IUCN (2019), *Red list of threatened species*, www.iucnredlist.org/.

Intergovernmental Science-Policy Platform on Biodiversity and Ecosystem Services (IPBES) (2019), Global Assessment Report on Biodiversity and Ecosystem Services, https://www.ipbes.net/global-assessment-report-biodiversity-ecosystem-services.

OECD (2019), "Biodiversity: Finance and the Economic and Business Case for Action, Report prepared for the G7 Environment Ministers' Meeting, 5-6 May 2019", http://www.oecd.org/env/resources/biodiversity/biodiversity-finance-and-the-economic-and-business-case-for-action.htm.

SCBD (2016), "Marine debris: Understanding, preventing and mitigating the significant adverse impacts on marine and coastal biodiversity", *CBD Technical Series No 83*, Secretariat of the Convention on Biological Diversity, https://www.cbd.int/doc/publications/cbd-ts-83-en.pdf.

UNEP (2019), "Chapter 6 Biodiversity" in *Global Environmental Outlook 6*, https://wedocs.unep.org/bitstream/handle/20.500.11822/27659/GEO6_CH6.pdf?sequence=1&isAllowed=y.

UNSD (2019), *The Sustainable Development Goals Report 2019*, https://unstats.un.org/sdgs/report/2019/The-Sustainable-Development-Goals-Report-2019.pdf.

UNEP-WCMC, IUCN and NGS (2018). *Protected Planet Report 2018*. UNEP-WCMC, IUCN and NGS: Cambridge UK; Gland, Switzerland; and Washington, D.C., USA. https://www.unep-wcmc.org/system/comfy/cms/files/files/000/001/445/original/Global_Protected_Planet_2018.pdf.

www.ingramcontent.com/pod-product-compliance
Lightning Source LLC
Chambersburg PA
CBHW051233200326
41519CB00025B/7353